A Game that Smiles

RICHIE BENNIS

WITH CIARÁN KENNEDY

www.**HERO**BOOKS.digital

HEROBOOKS

PUBLISHED BY HERO BOOKS
1 WOODVILLE GREEN
LUCAN
CO. DUBLIN
IRELAND

Hero Books is an imprint of Umbrella Publishing
First Published 2020
Copyright © Richie Bennis and Ciaran Kennedy 2020
All rights reserved

ISBN 9781910827093

Cover design and formatting: Jessica Maile
Ebook formatting: www.ebooklaunch.com
Photographs: Inpho, Sportsfile and the Bennis family collection

Dedication

To my rock, my wife Mary
(Behind every good man stands a better woman)

Contents

My Son

PROLOGUE

MY SON, DICKIE was born in July of 1973.

Two months later, the week of the All-Ireland final between Limerick and Kilkenny, we did not know if he would live.

I was preparing for the biggest game of my career, but at the same time a game of hurling was not my greatest concern. As you can imagine, it was not even close. And as the days to the game counted down, and the All-Ireland final got closer, and closer still, Dickie became very sick.

My wife, Mary and I did not know if he was going to pull through.

A few people close to me started hearing rumours that I wouldn't be playing in the game, and they questioned me, but not many people around the county knew the reason why my involvement was in doubt.

WE WENT UP to Dublin on the Saturday before the game, and at that time the wives and girlfriends of the players travelled with us as well. Mary and I had visited Dickie's doctor before heading off and he said everything was fine. He told me to go and play the game.

But I had no idea what I should do.

Some people whom I trusted were telling me that I would regret it if I didn't play in the biggest game in my life. I had been dreaming of playing in an All-Ireland final for as long as I could remember.

I knew I might never get a chance to play in another.

Finally, we decided that I would play. Off I went but, naturally, I left our home under a great cloud of worry and concern. Even after I had made the decision to make myself available, I still wasn't sure if I was in the right state of mind to play against Kilkenny.

On the train up to Dublin I was struggling to take my mind off things.

People were chatting to me about this and that, but it was all going in one ear and out the other. At one stage, I noticed a woman I knew, who was the wife of a county board official, making her way along the carriage. She was whispering something to people as she passed them by.

To me, she looked like a woman delivering bad news.

As she came nearer to where Mary and I were sitting, she stopped again at a small group of people and leaned in to them.

'Did you hear the news?

'... Richie's son is after dying.'

And off she went to find somebody else to tell.

I DON'T KNOW if my reaction was panic or shock.

Both, obviously.

I jumped out of my seat and went after her, but she had no way of clarifying if it was true or not. She told me that she had heard it from someone else, who heard it from someone else, and so on and so on.

My mind was swirling as I listened to her.

We had no phone to ring home. Mobile phones were decades away.

Mary and I had to sit back down, and we had to wait until the train pulled into Heuston Station in Dublin. Only then did we get to find out if our son was alive.

At one stage, the train had slowed because of delays. I felt like jumping off and running the rest of the way. When we eventually got to Dublin, I raced off to get to a phone.

I rang the hospital.

I could barely speak, but they assured us that it wasn't true. It had been a false rumour circulating on the train.

Someone had heard... 'Richie's son isn't well'.

Those words filtered through the carriages, and the words changed into... 'Richie's son is dying'.

Before long people were being told... 'Richie's son is dead!'

Everyone on our carriage was given this awful news. But the doctor on the other end of the line reassured myself and Mary that everything 'is okay'. He also said that he did not expect any significant developments in Dickie's condition over the weekend.

'Go off and play your match,' he instructed me.

I heard him, but I could not help asking myself one big question. *What on earth are Mary and I doing on the other side of the country?*

Even in the hotel that night I was keeping in regular contact with the hospital, but the news never changed.

'Everything is fine…

'Stop worrying Richie!'

Dr Basheer even gave me his home phone number so I could keep checking in on the day of the game, just to put my mind at rest. One of the Limerick trainers came up to me. He could see the turmoil written all over my face.

'Richie… if you have a problem and you're going to take it out with you onto Croke Park, I'd advise you not to go out.

'We badly need you,' he continued, 'but there are going to be 70,000 people in the stands who are not aware of your problem.'

It was a very decent thing to say, but I felt like flooring him.

After going through all that on the train, I had firmed up in my head that there wasn't a hope in hell that I wouldn't walk out onto that pitch.

I was on the wrong side of the country while my infant son was fighting for his life back in Limerick. But I was there for a reason.

OUR WIVES STAYED in different accommodation the night before the game. I was with the team in our hotel.

I was sitting on my bed in the hotel. It was around 11 o'clock, and we had come back to our rooms after a few of us had gone for a walk. Sleep, however, wasn't easy to come by with everything that was going on.

I wasn't the only one facing the predicament of a long night of sleeplessness. Nerves and excitement were getting the better of a few of the lads.

The fella in the room next to me, whose name I will not be sharing even all of these years later, could obviously here my fidgeting about the place.

There was a loud tap on my wall.

'I CAN'T SLEEP!' he shouted.

Feck this.

I got out of my bed, and I knocked into his room. I told him I was going down to the hotel bar. And I also told him that I'd be back with four pints.

Two for him.

Two for myself!

I fully realized that being seen with four pints of stout the night before an All-Ireland final might have taken any decision about playing in the game out of my hands. Stealth had to be key.

I made it down to the bar without any hassle.

I put the four pints on a tray and was carefully making my way back up to my room. Everything was going to plan. On the final stretch, I turned down one of the long corridors and there was Tom Boland.

The secretary of the county board was turning the other corner, at the far end of the corridor. Tom was a very anti-drink man at the best of times, so I knew I was in trouble. But there was a little bit of a recess in the wall beside me, and out of pure instinct I leaned up against it and made a woeful attempt at trying to hide my frame and my tray of pints.

I was like a sorry dog with a paw over my face.

I backed into the wall and the door behind me swung open. How I didn't fall flat on my back and drench myself with stout would turn out to be only the first miracle of the night. I turned around and there was an old lady sitting up in the bed.

I'm still not sure if she was saying the rosary or if she was knitting. She looked at me with this mix of bewilderment and fright.

Balancing my tray on one hand, I raised the other to my lips and gave her this manic… 'SSSSSHHHHHHHHHHHHHH'.

After taking in the scene that had just crashed through her door, she nodded at me in acknowledgement. Or maybe that was also fear. The two of us were frozen in silence.

I heard Tom slowly walk past.

After a few seconds I quietly thanked my short-term roommate and quickly tip-toed my way back to my own room. The lad next door wondered what took me so long.

'I'll explain some other time,' I told him. We both started into our two pints. Soon enough, the job done, the pair of us were out like a light. It was actually the best night's sleep that I had had in weeks.

THE MORNING OF the game, Dickie was the first thought on my mind as soon as I woke up. It was pouring rain, and before and after breakfast I was checking in with the doctor back home in Limerick.

Everything was still fine.

We were about to get on the bus to Croke Park and reception contacted us to say that a crowd of people from the North had sent us down 20 match tickets. They couldn't travel down because of The Troubles. That might only seem like a little event, but it stuck with me. It was a reminder that the whole country was invested in this game, and that we had support from all corners of Ireland.

For some reason Limerick hurling has always had a good following in Northern Ireland. Obviously, we all had tickets, so we gave the 20 to a garda and told him to give them to Limerick people looking for tickets outside the stadium.

God only knows what actually happened them.

We arrived into the stadium and got settled in our dressing-room. Before we took the pitch one of our trainers broke down making a great speech, which Éamonn Cregan then took on, and Frankie Nolan finished off.

There was nothing outstanding about what was said. It was just a simple message delivered well, which is all we needed at that stage. We were reminded of what we should do, how to approach it, and not to worry about the opposition.

The theory was if we all did our own job well, we would win.

My head was all over the place, but the weird thing was that what was happening my son had made the match pale into something approaching insignificance. Even though it was my life-long dream to play for Limerick in an All-Ireland final.

I knew it was a huge occasion, but Dickie's fight just put everything else into perspective. This was not the biggest sporting occasion in the country, or a day when you can make or break a reputation, or a day when the expectation of the entire county was on my shoulders.

Neither was it the biggest day of my life.

It was just a game of hurling.

Nothing more. Nothing less.

I WAS MORE relaxed than I had been for any game, club or county, that season. I told myself that it is just 70 minutes, no bother to me.

The knock on the door came.

'Time to go lads.'

I was never more ready.

I was braced to meet a mighty roar when we ran out the tunnel, which we did get, but my mind was still only on Dickie.

I felt nothing much.

I heard nothing.

The All-Ireland final was nothing to fear.

Our first born, Dickie was diagnosed with cerebral palsy a few months after his birth. He had no quality to his life. He barely had any movement.

Dickie was at home for his first six years before we had to make the difficult decision for him to get the best care outside of our home.

We were told that he would only live to his mid-20s, but our boy was a fighter. And what a fighter!

Dickie Bennis died when he was 36 years-old.

PART ONE

Awakenings

DIARMAID BYRNES
(Patrickswell and Limerick)

HURLING IN PATRICKSWELL is everything.

The hurling field itself is right in the heart of the village, and then Richie's family home is only around the corner from it. He's someone you always bump into around Patrickswell, whether you are just going down to the shop or up to the hurling field.

His connection with the club is just massive with his family and all his brothers. You get to know all of them through the club, and when you look at Richie, with everything that he's done in his career, not only is he known throughout the county, but he's known all over Ireland.

He's a massive character in Patrickswell.

Whenever you bump into him around the village the chat is always hurling. He's always intrigued about what is going on with Limerick, and he's always been good with advice, even if you just meet him in the shop.

He'd always be comparing things to how they were back in his day.

'Jaysus I remember when I was taking frees we wouldn't be doing that.'

Or, 'Sure when we were training we would do such and such'.

But it always comes with a word of advice.

Some of the stories he'd tell you... lads going into the shower at half-time to smoke a fag! You're telling him about going in to maybe have a Dioralyte and an energy gel or a sports drink, and he's going, 'Ah Jaysus... go way out of that'.

IT'S CRAZY HOW much it has changed. It's still an amateur sport obviously, but it has come so far. The game has gotten faster, the tactics are different and he's always intrigued to hear things about that.

We have to try to keep things in-house in the Limerick squad but you end up giving Richie a small bit because you just have so much respect for him.

You don't want to be telling Richie Bennis lies!

PATRICKSWELL IS A *very close knit club. When you go into our clubhouse, on the left hand side of the hall, we have the 20 club championship winning teams on the wall. We won the 20th this year, but it was those lads around the early 1970s who started all of that off for us. Richie, his brother Phil, Frankie Nolan, Sean Foley... they were the first big names from the club to go and represent Limerick. Then to go on and win Munster championships, the National league and an All-Ireland... like, Richie won 10 club championships with Patrickswell!*

These are the guys you're looking at when you're a young guy at the club. They set in stone what hurling means to Patrickswell and the tradition of hurling in the village.

We won the All-Ireland on Sunday, August 19, 2018. The interest levels in hurling absolutely soared around the county after that. It was incredible to witness going around to different clubs and functions for medal presentations or whatever. You could see the increase in the numbers and the amount of young kids now interested in hurling.

It was great to see that positive impact.

The Saturday after the game we had our own homecoming in Patrickswell. Richie, Phil, Frankie and Sean, the four lads from 1973, were all there, and then myself, Cian Lynch and Aaron Gillane were up on the stage.

Going to the hurling field where you learned your trade, alongside the two lads who you trained with, looking down and seeing the lads who had been there and done it in 1973 – we won't get into the fact we could have had a few more in 1994 and 1996 – but it was a very special occasion for the three of us.

And you could see that it brought back memories for the four lads from 1973.

That was probably the most special moment for us across those weeks.

« CHAPTER 1 »

THE CURSE OF the optimist is that you head into every new season with a sneaking feeling that this just might be Limerick's year, regardless of whatever evidence may be staring you in the face.

Being from Limerick, the All-Ireland is the Holy Grail, but the realist in all of us cautions that winning the championship is most likely going to be beyond us on any given year. That is often down to the talent elsewhere, just as much as it is down to what Limerick have themselves. All we ever want is to give it a good go. If the players hurl well, try their hardest, but get beaten by a better team?

Then, so be it.

We were one step away in 2007, but any sense of growth or development slowly disappeared; 2008 was just so flat. Under Justin McCarthy in 2009, the wheels had completely fallen off. The way he went about things when he came in really set the whole thing back a few years. That group were never going to go anywhere under him after such a disruptive start.

He did the right thing, but made a complete mess of things with the way he did it. His time in charge started off on a very bad note.

After all the chaos of how he went about dropping players, a few of the lads got together and decided that they wouldn't play for him. It turned into a players' strike. Instead of trying to get back to their best, we were sitting there watching statements come out and hearing all sorts of different rumours.

I found the whole episode quite disheartening.

I felt sorry for the lads. I knew what they were capable of, and I knew them all to be good, honest lads. It wasn't pleasant to see things play out like that in the media, and to see the way the group fell apart. I just wish they had made more of an effort to get it sorted out internally. For it to be all over the newspapers, it kind of puts a black mark on that period for Limerick, and it can give lads a bad name. The county board should have stepped in and gotten it sorted before it all came to a head.

Naturally, it was no surprise when Justin walked away in 2010. Limerick had been relegated to Division 2 after losing all of their league games that year, and were hammered out the gate by Cork in Munster before losing to Offaly in the qualifiers. We were going nowhere with the way Justin was managing the team.

I think he got the job at the wrong time too. He had come into Limerick on the back of seven years with Waterford. He had brought Waterford far as he could have, and I think he was at the end of his tether.

Limerick got a tired Justin at a time when they needed someone fresh and hungry. That showed on the pitch. I had to remind myself that there was nothing I could do about it.

My time was up.

MAYBE IT WAS just as well I wasn't reappointed as manager.

I had loved the job but there was no denying the fact that it was stressful, and probably more so than I had noticed, or let myself acknowledge.

Two weeks after it was confirmed that I wasn't staying on as Limerick manager, I was inside in the Regional Hospital in the city having a routine check-up. Afterwards I was chatting away to one of the doctors I knew.

He was a fierce man for hurling. After a few minutes chatting he was asking about my health in general, and inquired if I had ever gone for a colonoscopy. I didn't even know what it was he was asking me.

He told me that it was a good thing to do at my age, so I said no bother. He booked me in to come back for a colonoscopy a few days later.

I WENT IN, and went through the process. It was all very straightforward. Answer a few questions, get into the robe, and then they whisked me off.

It was all over in a flash.

The amazing thing is they give you the results straight away. Now bear in mind that a few days previously I didn't know what a colonoscopy was. Now here I was sitting in the waiting room, finishing off my bit of tea, and realising the bad news the minute I saw the doctor's face when he came into the room.

Most of the information went in one ear and out the other. When you hear cancer, you assume that's it.

I couldn't make sense of it.

I thought I was fighting fit.

We went through everything quickly. The sooner they operated, the better my chances. I told them let's operate now. They booked me in for the next day.

I left, got into the car, and cried the whole way home.

Bowel cancer.

At my age.

This was it.

I stopped off at the butcher and bought the biggest T-bone steak he had. I got home, and sat Mary down to deliver the news. The two of us sat in the living room and cried for the night. It was one of the longest evenings of my life. I was scared for myself, but I was also scared for Mary.

I didn't want to leave her on her own.

We eventually tried to get to sleep, but I'd say I never gave the bedroom ceiling such an examination.

I WENT BACK into the hospital the next morning and went under the knife. Every minute of that morning felt like an hour, but before I knew it I was coming back to my senses in the waiting room.

They had removed around 12 inches of the lining of my bowel. It hadn't gone inside the boundary of the bowel yet. It was confined, which made the whole thing much more straightforward for the doctors. They said they were happy enough and that I was good to go home.

About two hours after we got home, the phone rang.

It was one of the doctors.

The operation had been a success, and I was cleared of any symptoms.

It was hard to wrap my head around at first. As far as I knew, I had had cancer for one day. Twenty-four hours after getting the bad news, I was back at home as if nothing had happened, ready to get on with life. Though six months of precautionary chemotherapy followed.

I knew I was one of the lucky ones. Thank God I was sent for that colonoscopy, as timing is key with those things. When I had the time to soak it all in I realised that I probably did have some symptoms in the weeks and months beforehand, but they weren't things that I would have connected with cancer at all. I thought they were just things that came along with old age.

For anyone reading this, just go and get checked because you never know. I went back in for another colonoscopy six months later, and was still worried that they might discover they missed something, but everything has been fine since, thank God.

If I had been reappointed manager in 2008, there is a good chance I would have blamed the pressure of the position for my illness. Stepping back from the game hadn't really been on my radar, but that scare quickly brought into focus the fact there are more important things in life. It helped me accept the fact that I wasn't going to be involved with Limerick anymore.

Maybe not reappointing me was a good turn the county board did for me. I was ready to resume life in the stands.

IT WAS A frustrating few years for Limerick supporters. There seemed to be a lot of chopping and changing, and no real sense of consistency.

Dónal O'Grady was the next man in after Justin.

He brought a bit of discipline and a bit of stability to the situation. He had won an All-Ireland with Cork, so had good pedigree as a manager. He did well with Limerick, but I don't think his style of hurling suited our players, and I feel that's what ultimately held them back.

There were a few players Dónal kept on the panel that weren't able to adapt to his style. Take Brian Geary for example, a player who had been on the Limerick panel for years. Brian had been a classic centre-back, a proper no-nonsense, long-clearances sort of player.

All of a sudden Dónal was looking for him to play short passes in a sort of possession game, and it didn't suit him at all. He wasn't the only one having that problem.

Limerick still did well under Dónal. I think he might have benefited from mixing things up a bit more. Instead of completely going for a short-passing game, he might have been wiser to simply integrate it into the way players were used to playing.

In 2011 we lost by a point to Waterford in the Munster semi-final and reached the All-Ireland quarter-finals through the qualifiers. We lost to Dublin down in Thurles, 3-13 to 0-18.

It was a game we should never have lost, and again it was down to the style of hurling. To be fair to Dónal, he had been successful with that style of play with Cork, but the difference was he had the players for it with them. Newtownshandrum won a club All-Ireland in 2004 with that style of play, and players from that team like Jerry and Ben O'Connor were key men in Dónal's Cork team. It gave him a base to work from, whereas in Limerick he was starting from scratch introducing lads to a whole new game plan.

Overall, Dónal did alright with Limerick, particularly given the circumstances when he took the job, but he left in 2011, with John Allen taking over on a two-year term.

I THOUGHT JOHN Allen was a big asset to Limerick hurling. It was kind of funny that he followed Dónal in Limerick. Not only were both from St Finbarr's in Cork, but John had also succeeded Dónal as Cork boss back in 2004. He had done really well with Cork, winning the All-Ireland in 2005 and losing the 2006 final by three points to Kilkenny.

He did great work with Limerick. In terms of style, he kept a little bit of what Dónal had been doing but blended it with the more typical Limerick approach. It worked a treat, and was easier for the players to grasp. It was a bit more natural for them.

It's not that the players were limited, but when you are playing a certain way with your club – as most of the Limerick lads were – it's very difficult to come in and do something totally different with the county. You can't just flick that on and off like a switch.

In all, 2012 was forgetful enough.

It was a tough ask for John's first year. We lost to Tipperary in the first round of the Munster championship, and went in through the back door again. Limerick scored 8-26 against Antrim in the first round of the qualifiers. Shane Dowling scored 4-9 that day, which was three points more than Antrim scored in total.

The game was a bit of a joke. Limerick were 4-1 to 0-2 ahead after just 10 minutes. They then beat Clare and lost by three goals to Kilkenny in the All-Ireland quarter-finals. It wasn't a bad return. On another year, if the only games you lost were to Tipperary and Kilkenny, there would be a decent chance that you would have reached the Munster and All-Ireland finals.

We came back stronger in 2013. Limerick beat Tipperary by three points in the Munster semi-final in the Gaelic Grounds and played Cork in the Munster final.

It was a wonderful day.

The game was fixed for the Gaelic Grounds again. Limerick hadn't been in a Munster final for six years. You could sense heading into the stadium that day that it was going to be a special occasion. I could feel it in the air.

We won it convincingly enough in the end, 0-24 to 0-15. Pat Horgan was sent off for Cork just before half-time after catching Paudie O'Brien under a high ball, but to be honest I don't think it had that much of a bearing on the outcome. Limerick were already moving well when he was sent off.

We played some great hurling, and you could see there was a real sense of spirit again in the way they played. It was Limerick's first Munster title for 17 years.

I was one of the many who invaded the pitch afterwards to watch the lads lift the cup. It's a memory I treasure still.

My only real complaint with John Allen's tenure would be the way he handled the subsequent All-Ireland semi-final. We played Clare in Croke Park, and when Clare started to pull away Limerick didn't do enough to try and rein them back in. John accepted defeat in that game, and the fact that it was against Clare only poured salt on the wound.

It looked to me as if he felt his job was done after winning Munster. That anything else would have been a bonus. There was plenty of time to try and change that game but on the sideline John didn't show any of the passion that he had in the Munster final.

That didn't sit well with me at all.

That's also one of the biggest problems with having a manager from outside the county. They can set goals based on their interpretation of the county's limits, and then feel that they have taken them as far as they can.

A manager from the county will always want more, and always hold that little bit more belief, because at the end of the day you're a supporter too. That's the main reason I could have never seen myself managing a county other than Limerick. A manager from outside the county will always be under more scrutiny, and won't get the same amount of patience from supporters as someone from within the county.

John was Limerick's third successive manager from Cork, and that didn't go unnoticed around Limerick.

People were questioning why we were always looking outside of our own county, and whether we were producing people good enough ourselves.

IT WAS A fair question. The success John Allen brought helped, but people were delighted when TJ Ryan, a Limerick man through and through, took over from him.

I like TJ. He had been part of Dónal's backroom set-up, so was a familiar face to the players. We had been going through managers every season or two, and there was a sense that TJ would at least have ambitions of staying in the job for a few years. Others were maybe using the job as a stepping stone, but TJ had a real passion for Limerick hurling.

I knew TJ well. His brother, Donie had been on the panel when I was Limerick manager, and TJ himself had been too, albeit very briefly. When we lost to Cork by a point in 2006, TJ retired in the dressing room after the game.

He had been playing as full-back, and he wasn't really comfortable there. He was being played out of position to plug a hole rather than getting the best out of himself in his proper position. That said, I actually thought he did well as a full-back.

Anyway, I think he was rather relieved when I took the No. 3 jersey off him and put him up at left half-forward.

Still, he decided to retire after the Cork game, and I thought that was fair enough. I didn't think I'd be staying on as manager so who was I to tell him to give it a few more years? Had I known I'd be hanging around for another while yet I would have 100 per cent tried to change his mind. He would have been a real asset.

I met him a few years later and got the feeling he would have stayed on if I had asked him to come back; that retiring was almost a spur of the moment thing.

Even in the short amount of time I worked with TJ, you would have been able to pick him out as a future manager. He had a good mind for the game. He did very well as Limerick manager too, even if he didn't end up with the silverware to show for it. He was originally meant to be joint manager with Dónal, who had agreed to come back, but in typical Limerick fashion we handled it wrong.

There was a county board meeting where someone claimed that Dónal and TJ had 'apologised for the abysmal' performances during the league that year. The two lads insisted that they had done no such thing. They had finished second in Division 1B despite only coming on board late the previous year.

Dónal walked away, while TJ agreed to stay on. This all happened at the end of April. A complete shambles.

It made the job TJ did all the more impressive. They lost the Munster final to Cork and then played Kilkenny in the All-Ireland semi-final. Limerick dominated Kilkenny for much of the game but Kilkenny struck two goals at crucial stages in the game. To hold Kilkenny to just 13 points and not win was cruel. The second goal came from a dropping ball into the square when we had them on the ropes. It could have gone anywhere but went into the Limerick net.

One of those things.

It was like they didn't really recover from that game. They were well beaten by Tipperary in the Munster semi-final the following year, and then lost by a point to Dublin in the qualifiers. Then they lost to Tipp at the same stage the next year, before Clare dumped them out of the qualifiers.

TJ had taken them as far as he could at that stage, and he admitted as much himself when he decided to step down. The last few years didn't go the way TJ would have wanted but he can be proud of the work he did.

« CHAPTER 2 »

THE YEARS FLY by. Before I knew it, it had been a decade since I was Limerick manager, and we appeared to be no closer to bridging the gap.

I didn't know too much about John Kiely when he took the job after the 2016 championship. What did intrigue me was the fact that he actually requested it. Straight away that told me that he saw something in the players. That he felt there was some untapped potential there.

I knew that feeling.

John took the job at a time when Limerick were kind of at a crossroads. We had pushed on a bit over the previous couple of years but there was always a danger of slipping back down the pack if things weren't done properly. There is often a feeling around Limerick hurling that things can quite quickly go one way or the other.

They didn't make any great impression in 2017. After a very mixed league campaign, they lost to Clare down in Thurles in the Munster semi-final and then went out to Kilkenny in the first round of the qualifiers. It was a tough hand to be dealt, but that's the reality of championship hurling. Nothing ever comes easy.

Welcome to management, John.

There was no real sense of excitement around the county ahead of 2018. It was the usual sort of talk. We had a good core of really talented hurlers, and some really honest hard workers, but the general consensus was probably that we were a bit limited in too many areas to really compete.

FROM WHAT I saw in the early stages of the year, the same old problems were still there.

Limerick were in Division 1B of the league, and I went to all of the matches. They hammered Laois on the opening weekend, and were even more comfortable away to Offaly. They beat Dublin and Antrim too, but the scorelines didn't tell the full story.

I felt that the team was struggling to find some rhythm. There were flashes of quality, then long periods where Limerick faded out of games. That stuff would kill a team in the championship.

My mind changed on March 11, the day they played Galway up in Salthill, the first real challenge they had had. Limerick were slow starters again that day. Cathal Mannion scored an early goal for Galway and within three minutes they were beating us, 1-3 to 0-0. We were eight points down at half-time, despite Galway resting a bunch of their key men.

The performances were driving me mad. We had so much talent there but for whatever reason they couldn't turn out consistent performances. I turned to Mary and said, 'Typical Limerick... here we go again'. I was thinking about another summer of disappointment ahead.

All promise, no product.

To make matters worse, Galway brought on five or six of their best players for the second-half. I was worried about just how bad the final score might be. Yet to be fair to the lads, they dug in after half-time.

David Reidy hit a point, and Aaron Gillane scored three frees in-a-row.

This was more like it.

They looked determined. They looked hungry. Coming up to 50 minutes, Kyle Hayes hit a goal that left just a point between the teams. A few more points were traded and then Cian Lynch put us ahead for the first time in the game with two minutes to play, before Pat Ryan struck the insurance point.

Out of nowhere, Limerick had turned it around.

The result secured promotion, meaning we would be back playing in the top tier of the league for the first time since 2010. Back where we belong.

That day, my opinion of the team was completely transformed, and it wasn't just down to the fact that they produced such an impressive comeback. It was down to the manner in which they did it. Not once did it look like Limerick were panicking.

Even when Galway threw in Joe Canning and a handful of other front-liners, Limerick just stuck at it. They didn't go hitting long balls, or desperately trying to find goals. They just kept hurling to the structure that they had started the game with, and in the second-half it began to work for them.

You could see it just... CLICK.

Even after taking such a hammering in the first-half, they didn't lose faith in their system and the way they wanted to play the game.

That to me was the sign of a tight unit. It indicated that they were all fully invested in the manager's plan, and had total faith in each other to make it work – even when all the signs were pointing to a complete thrashing. After being so concerned at half-time, I was almost in shock come the final whistle.

I turned to Mary again.

'Jesus... they might actually be on to something here.'

I HAD GENUINELY been worried about where Limerick's season was headed. That might sound silly given we topped the group and won all of our games, but results don't always tell the full story.

In those first four games against Laois, Offaly, Dublin and Antrim, I just didn't feel Limerick had shown any real signs that there was anything different about them. Some people would say it's only the league, but you can still often get a sense of how a team is building during that period. Limerick to me looked alright, but there wasn't anything there that looked overly exciting.

That all changed after beating Galway.

Next up was a win against Clare in the league quarter-finals. It took the novelty of a free-taking competition to separate the sides after extra-time. It was a cruel way to decide a game, but both sides had given everything, and with Limerick beating Clare in the league for the first time in seven years, I wasn't complaining.

Tipperary beat us in the semi-final by a goal, but there was no real arguing with the outcome. It was a good contest between two good sides. Sometimes the game just doesn't go your way.

Jason Forde scored 2-11 for Tipp that day, but it was pleasing to see Limerick have 13 different scorers. I had a feeling that the summer was going to be even more interesting than I had previously thought.

I HEADED ALONG to the first game in the Munster championship against Tipperary in the Gaelic Grounds, and I did not really know what to expect.

The league already felt like quite some time ago. You start questioning your thinking. Maybe I had become overly optimistic during the latter stages of the league. Maybe the other teams had been holding back a bit and that had allowed Limerick to look better than we actually were.

I had enough experience to know that championship hurling is a completely different animal. Any number of different scenarios ran through my head on the way to the stadium.

Tipp were a good team, but I was confident that Limerick were brewing something special. By the time I reached the Gaelic Grounds I was convinced we would beat them. Admittedly, I never have any fear when we're playing Tipp, no matter what shape Limerick are in.

I'm not sure why that is.

But I know there are plenty of Limerick supporters who feel the same way. It doesn't matter how much better Tipp are playing in the build-up or what might be going wrong with Limerick, we've always been able to give them a game.

We've often beaten them when, on paper, they're far superior to us. They're just one of those teams that don't really strike any fear into Limerick people.

I felt the same when I was playing.

Maybe they feel the same way about us.

As it happened, we beat them and beat them well.

1-23 to 2-16.

Again, I was impressed with the way the responsibly of scoring was spread across the team. We had nine different scorers, whereas they only had five.

We were clearly the better team in every department, and the crowd could sense that from fairly early on. Limerick were a point down at half-time but nobody was too worried. They lifted it in the second-half. Tipp should have come out and tried to stretch their lead, but they looked cautious. That allowed Limerick to really attack the game, and they dictated the whole thing from there on, winning by four points.

Next up was Cork.

Whatever my feeling about Tipp, Cork are a totally different proposition. You never know what will happen in a game against Cork, largely because you get the sense that they don't know what will happen themselves.

They must be the most unpredictable county in hurling.

Every year, they could either make a real stab at winning the All-Ireland or they could go out and look like they haven't got a clue what they are meant to be doing. It would drive me mad to support them, let alone play for them.

Aaron Gillane was sent off after less than 30 minutes following a stupid tangle with Seán O'Donoghue. Thank God he learned his lesson that day.

Cork were the better team. With the hurlers they have, and us only having 14 men for most of the game, they should have put us to bed. The game was there for them. I was surprised that they didn't try to play more sensible, possession hurling. They just kept it all a bit loose, and again Limerick produced a really good second-half performance and finished the game strongly to get a draw.

I thought it was a great result for us, given the circumstances. I think that result did a lot for the confidence that the Limerick public had in them too.

A man down.

Away from home.

And they just kept at it, worked hard and got a result. I'm sure it also gave the players massive belief.

WATERFORD HAD TO concede home venue for our next game because Walsh Park had been deemed unfit for use, and I don't think their heads were fully right.

We easily beat them.

It was no contest really, and the result was beyond doubt by half-time. The downside of that was that it was dreadful preparation for what lay around the corner, a trip to Ennis to face Clare. Few teams leave Ennis with a result at the best of times.

We barely fired a shot and got an unmerciful beating, losing by 11 points. Still, it didn't change my own belief that the team were on the right path. We didn't hurl well, but many good teams have had off-days in Ennis.

Just a blip, I told myself.

In hindsight, that result was the best thing to happen Limerick all summer long. We played Carlow in the All-Ireland preliminary quarter-finals. It was the perfect game to get back on the horse. For the first 15 minutes Carlow gave us as much of a game as anyone else had up to that point, but it didn't take long for Limerick to settle and the gulf in quality soon became clear.

KILKENNY, OF COURSE, was going to be the real acid test of whether or not this Limerick team meant business. Again, I was confident that we would win, particularly because the game was in Thurles.

Take Kilkenny out of Croke Park and you always have a better chance. They love Croke Park, just like the Dublin footballers and the great Kerry teams. They just know it so well that it feels like home to them.

We started well, but all of a sudden Kilkenny nabbed a goal and we were a point down.

The little doubts start to creep in then.

Here we go again?

At least we reached mid-July!

Then Tom Morrissey caught a ball.

He soloed in… and drove it over the bar, and we ended up beating them. It's funny the little moments that happen during a season that stick with you.

After the full-time whistle, a Kilkenny supporter turned around to me.

She took a deep breath.

Then she spoke up.

'By God… Galway have a handy All-Ireland this year!'

She can be thankful my wife was with me, otherwise I would have offered my own opinion in no uncertain terms.

Limerick got a lot right that day. TJ Reid was very well curtailed. He still hit seven points, but that's a quiet day by his standards. Again, we just never deviated from the game plan. Someone told me that Paul Kinnerk, the Limerick trainer, was asked what their Plan B was going to be if things weren't going their way?

'Improve on Plan A', was his reply, I'm told.

That's exactly what Limerick were doing. If the game looked like it was getting away from them, they just worked harder, and raised the intensity.

And ran themselves into the ground.

THE SEMI-FINAL against Cork was the one game I really dreaded. We had a dreadful record against Cork in the championship.

We had beaten them in the 2013 Munster final, which somehow was the last time we played them, but before that we had only beaten them once in the seven previous meetings. It turned out to be a phenomenal game.

Sixty-eight scores and extra-time.

Something happened that day. With the game in the balance, I felt there was a little sign this would be our year.

The official attendance was flashed up on the big screen... 71,073.

I could see by the reaction around me that I wasn't the only Limerick supporter who recognised the significance of the '73', the last year we won the All-Ireland. It's one of those things that gets into your head.

I had been spotting little omens all year.

My daughter had got a new car, and the number on the registration was 1973. If I was ever seen driving that around, people would have thought I'd lost the plot completely.

Also, in 1973 Eamon De Valera was President.

A Limerick man.

Since we claim Michael D Higgins, I was banking that as another link.

WE WERE TWO points up by half-time, and had stretched it out to six with about seven minutes to go. 'We need a goal!' I told Mary.

It was the only way we'd really kill off Cork.

Then Nicky Quaid had his moment. Instantly, no matter what happened Limerick, you knew it would be one of those clips that gets replayed again and again.

It was iconic.

Some people say it wasn't a save, some said it was a tackle.

I called it a three-in-one.

A save, a tackle and a pass, because Declan Hannon collected the ball after Quaid flicked it away. Whatever you want to call it, it was magic, racing out to nick the ball off Séamus Harnedy, the Cork forward bearing down on goal.

It won the match for us. I was right in line with it, and had a great view. It's one of those moments that you remember picture perfect.

I was convinced Harnedy was in for his goal.

It was a remarkable piece of goalkeeping. That said, what impressed me most was what was happening just behind Quaid. If Harnedy had squeezed the ball past him, there were three more Limerick bodies in line with him, waiting to try block the shot.

It was only on second viewing that I realised it was the three Limerick half-backs. I'm not sure any moment summed up the workrate that defined the team better than that. They never looked back after that moment.

In extra time, Dowling was pushed in the back and won a penalty. He dusted himself down and struck it himself. The subs worked well for us that day, because they were all of high quality. You always know that the Limerick bench has the ability to change a game.

Half of the Limerick bench could comfortably hold down a starting place on most teams. Dowling scored 1-4 having come on in the 56th minute.

Shortly after Dowling's penalty, Pat Ryan scored the cheekiest goal I've ever seen in Croke Park. After chasing what appeared to be a lost cause down in the right hand corner in front of Hill 16, he flicked the ball along the ground – a lovely moment for the old-school ground hurling fans – and turned Damien Cahalane inside out. From a tight angle, and with Cork goalkeeper, Anthony Nash advancing, he flicked the ball up onto his stick and tapped it over Nash's head.

That type of ingenuity and creativity is what makes hurling so special. Even though they were yet to win anything, John Kiely had his team playing with such confidence.

They had all the ingredients to win an All-Ireland.

Workrate, quality, confidence, and the ability to back it up. In my time, you might have 10 good players, and then five really high quality guys, who would more or less carry the team. Limerick now had top class players all over the pitch.

We beat Cork 3-32 to 2-31.

It was an absolutely magical day.

Limerick were back in the All-Ireland final, and anything felt possible.

« CHAPTER 3 »

ORIGINALLY, I WASN'T convinced that John Kiely was the right man for the job. I didn't know a whole lot about him. He came from a football background, but he had been on the panel in 1996.

There were three people picked to decide upon the Limerick set-up. I knew one of them, a very successful businessman who absolutely loves his hurling. He was the type of man that was taking on fellas during the recession, rather than letting men go.

Giving people a chance.

I knew that he was the type of man who could tell when someone has the qualities to be successful, in any walk of life. They got the right men to pick the set-up. Genuine hurling men with no agendas or biases.

They felt that appointing Kiely was a no-brainer.

THE BUZZ AROUND the county began as soon as Limerick won the semi-final. In my house questions about tickets started pouring in.

There's 13 of us in the family, and as it happens all the offspring are also mad into hurling. Tickets are a disaster when it comes to our family. I ended up being very lucky. I was doing a few interviews for RTÉ and got a ticket from them. I also did the Legends GAA Tour of Croke Park the day before the final, and I got two tickets through that as well.

I was probably busier in those few weeks leading up to the game than I had been when I was preparing for the All-Ireland as a player. Papers were ringing me up every day looking for opinions and comments on this and that, and I had to be very careful with what I said.

BENNIS PUTS PRESSURE ON LIMERICK

Or, worse.

BENNIS SAYS IT'S LIMERICK'S TO LOSE

Anything that could be interpreted as disruptive or unhelpful, in whatever comments I might make. Mary was great at making sure I didn't say anything I shouldn't.

You could also tell that the excitement had spread well beyond Limerick. People from all over the country bought into the novelty factor of having Limerick in the final.

September, 2007 seemed an age ago.

The county was starved for success.

Naturally enough, Galway were favourites. They were the reigning champions, and knew what it took to win on the biggest occasion in the hurling calendar.

IT'S A STRANGE experience attending an All-Ireland final, especially when Limerick are involved. As I made my way into Croke Park the memories just came flooding back.

They hit me out of nowhere.

I was thinking about how we were underdogs ourselves back in 1973. Limerick hadn't won an All-Ireland for 33 years at that stage. Now here we were, underdogs again, with no All-Ireland title for 45 years.

The similarities were startling, and that only made me spot more little coincidences. I looked at the names of the three Patrickswell lads in the match day programme.

Frankie Nolan was corner-forward for us in 1973, wearing the No.13 jersey. Now you had Aaron Gillane togging out at 13.

Cian Lynch was at No.8 in the middle of the field.

My old position back in '73.

Diarmaid Byrnes had varied between the No. 5 and No. 7 jerseys all season.

We had my brother, Phil and Sean Foley wearing 5 and 7 on our team.

Not only was the Patrickswell connection there, they were all wearing the same numbered shirts as us. As they say, the more things change…

OBVIOUSLY, CROKE PARK in its current guise is a world away from the stadium we knew in our playing days.

It's so much bigger and grander.

Yet, when you look out at that pitch… it's as if nothing has changed at all. It still feels like the same old place, even if the surface we played on would be labelled a disgrace by the modern players.

It's hard for me to put into words.

There's just a certain feeling about the place that never changes.

We came up the day beforehand because I was doing the Legends Tour, which is when they get a former footballer or hurler to lead a tour of the stadium, and tell a few yarns. It was great fun, mainly because of the people who turned up.

I had about 10 relations at it, but besides that there were Limerick and Galway people who were full of craic. And even though you're meant to be the tour guide, I found out things I never knew about the place.

I always thought Hill 16 was built from the rubble of the 1916 rising, which it wasn't! I won't give out any more little nuggets or business might take a dip.

The highlight was probably having John Hunt on the tour. John was 98 years old, and had flown home from Chicago for the final. You might have seen him the night before the final on *Up For The Match*, and he was also featured on the RTÉ news the following week. John had a lifelong friend with him to push him around in his wheelchair.

He told me about watching Limerick beat Kilkenny in the 1936 final, and about asking his doctor if he was okay to fly home for this final.

'When you get up in the air,' the doc replied, '… you may as well stay going until you see the shiny gates.'

John had some brilliant stories. A lovely man. I was very sad to hear of his passing a few months later. I'm glad his last trip home was worth it.

THAT NIGHT WE stayed in the Croke Park Hotel.

There were a lot of familiar faces knocking around. Jackie Tyrrell from Kilkenny was there, as was Seamus Harnedy from Cork. Tyrrell said he didn't see any way that Limerick could beat Galway. I took it as very arrogant.

Not for the first time, a gentle kick in the leg from Mary reminded me to just bite my lip. I thought to myself... *We'll see tomorrow.* It's gas how much those things stick with you, but to be honest they're the conversations that make the whole build-up so much fun.

It would be awful dull if we all agreed with each other all the time. Mind you, it's fair to say that Tyrrell knows what it takes to win an All-Ireland. He's entitled to his opinion. I just thought he was way off. Had he not seen Limerick hurl at all that summer?

Prior to the match I had been part of an interview with Galway's Cyril Farrell, who was the last manager to win two in-a-row, outside of Brian Cody. I told him he'd still have that record by the end of the day.

I was very confident about Limerick's chances.

First of all, I felt we had a stronger panel that Galway. We had lads who could come on, and you knew the performance levels wouldn't drop. That was one of our great strengths. Also, I had met many of the players in the weeks leading up to the game, and not one of them seemed in any way anxious or nervous about the game.

I got the sense that they felt if they turned up and hurled as they had all summer, they would be All-Ireland champions.

There was a real air of confidence off them, and not in any arrogant kind of way. I was quite impressed by it really, especially for such a young team. For most of them, this was their first All-Ireland final.

Maybe they're all just good actors?

We've a fine tradition of that too down in Limerick.

They had played in minor finals, of course. Maybe losing minor finals is a better way of preparing for senior level then coming in with All-Ireland medals in your pockets. You're always going to be more hungry if you haven't tasted that success before.

The Limerick team that won the three in-a-row at under-21 level, I got the impression they felt they had enough work behind them. That a senior All-Ireland was almost a guarantee.

I knew this new group didn't feel that way.

I felt myself becoming increasingly excited for them. They were heading into what would be one of the most special days of their lives.

By the end of those 80 minutes, everything could change for them.

« CHAPTER 4 »

IT WAS A game that was as thrilling as the days that counted down to it.

Limerick struck a few good early scores. Galway came back into it. They moved a point up after 15 minutes with a brilliant score, Joseph Cooney striking it over from way out after a magnificent catch from Gearóid McInerney.

Next Limerick attack, Graeme Mulcahy scored one of the scrappiest goals you will ever see in an All-Ireland final, but his persistence summed up the Limerick work ethic. We put a load of pressure on the Galway defence as they tried to clear their lines from a sideline cut, and eventually turned the ball over.

Kyle Hayes pinged a ball across to Mulcahy. The ball dropped loose as he turned his man, but Mulcahy kept at it, flicking the bobbling sliothar along the ground. And by the time he squeezed it past James Skehill, the Galway goalkeeper, there were four Galway defenders scrambling around trying to clear the danger.

It was a sort of bizarre goal, but when you get a break like that it can really feel like things are going to go your way.

THE CONFIDENCE OOZED out of the team after that.

They had come to play their way. The next score was magnificent. Declan Hannon burst out from centre-back to pick a ball from right under the nose of Joe Canning, and fired it over the bar.

He scored another from almost the same spot five minutes later which put Limerick five clear, with all 1-8 coming from play. Galway hit a few in reply.

But we were ahead, 1-10 to 0-9 at half-time.

Limerick hit five of the next six scores after the restart. We were 1-15 to 0-10 up with 50 minutes played, but Galway then hit the next two points.

Despite Limerick still being in the lead, it felt as though Galway were just about to really get going. Then we scored another goal.

This one was straight out of the 'School of Kiely'.

Galway's Gearóid McInerney picked up a ball facing his own goal on the '21', but was immediately put under fierce pressure by Tom Morrissey. Tom managed to win the ball, and gather it.

He cut inside.

And then showed great composure to find the net. It was a wonderful piece of individual work.

2-15 to 0-12.

We were flying.

GALWAY KEPT AT it, of course, and rattled off a few more scores.

Enter Shane Dowling.

Shane had been Limerick's super-sub, and filled the role again with the third goal in the final minutes. The best thing about that goal was that by putting Limerick eight points clear, the supporters could actually savour those final few minutes.

At least until they flashed up eight minutes of injury time.

We were nine points up.

Galway brought it back to seven.

Then our full-forward, Peter Casey was fouled. It should have been a yellow card, and a penalty. But you often don't get those decisions when a team is seven points up.

The referee let it go.

The ball was cleared.

And at the other end Conor Whelan scored a goal for Galway.

ALL OF A sudden it was just a four-point game.

Joe Canning popped over a 21 yard free.

We got a point.

They got a point.

And, incredibly… there was just a point in it.

AGAIN, THERE WAS a contentious free given close to the end.

One of those ones that are never given when the game is tied.

The way Limerick hurl, they crowd a player to try and force the turnover. I've watched it back countless times and I still don't see how Galway got a free.

Anyway, these things happen in hurling.

Up steps Canning again.

To this day, I'm convinced he didn't go for it.

From taking frees myself, and going off the way he was taking frees, there was no conviction in his strike. As well as that, Micheál Donoghue, the Galway manager, came out with a towel and the pair of them had a short conversation.

I suspect he told Canning to lob it in and hope for a deflection, or a free or whatever. It hit the back of the net. Despite being in control for practically the entire game, Limerick were on the ropes.

I was really enjoying the game until Galway had started to come back into it. I certainly wasn't the only one who had those heartbreaking scenes from the 1994 All-Ireland final flashing before my eyes.

Surely… not again?

When Galway had pulled it back to four points, and had all the momentum, Limerick were still playing their possession hurling. I loved the fact that they never deviated from what had served them so well, but there were plenty of agitated supporters around me screaming at them.

'CLEAR IT'

'HIT THE FUCKING BALL!!'

'JAYSUS… GET RID OF IT!!!!'

MARY IS NORMALLY a decent spectator, but she couldn't even look at it now. One Limerick lad stood up in front of us and turned around to the others who were shouting.

'For fuck sake…

'We're 45 years hitting the ball… and we've won… NOTHING!'

Dead right, I thought.

WE WERE SITTING right down near the pitch, along the half-way line.

You can almost feel the hits down there.

In the sixth minute of injury time Galway were only that point behind, and had all the momentum. My heart felt like it was about to burst through my shirt.

Graeme Mulcahy hit a beauty of a point from under the Cusack Stand to provide a bit of security, but Galway still had time for one more.

Please…

PLEASEEEEEEEE.

The last few moments were just mayhem.

I didn't even notice the full-time whistle had gone at first.

I thought the ref was just blowing for a free. I was wondering why the Limerick fans were getting so excited about this bloody free.

Then I saw the reaction of the players out on the pitch.

It struck me.

We've done it!

Despite dominating for so long we ended up being lucky to win, but nobody cared. The famine was over.

YOU NEVER KNOW how you're going to react in those situations.

I certainly didn't expect to cry, but there I was.

Standing in Croke Park, looking out at this remarkable bunch of young athletes, with tears in my eyes. I wasn't alone.

I FELT RELIEF.

Relief more than joy.

We had reached the promised land.

I felt as if all of my birthdays had come together.

A Galway fella behind me, who hadn't said a word to me all day, tapped me on the shoulder. 'Richie… I'm glad for you.'

He shook my hand.

They knew what it felt like. They had been there themselves not too long ago. We had a great time with any Galway supporters we chatted to after the game. There was no ill-feeling at all. You could see they were genuinely happy to see Limerick finally get over the line. I think there are a lot of counties who understand what it's like, and we're always happy to see an underdog reach the top of the mountain.

Even if I remove my green-tinted glasses, you instantly knew that it was one of those iconic All-Ireland wins. Some finals fade into obscurity, but people will remember Limerick in 2018.

There were just so many layers to it.

Even hearing *Dreams* by The Cranberries ring around the stadium, with all the Limerick supporters singing along, just a few months after Dolores O'Riordan had tragically passed at such a young age.

Her voice became the soundtrack to that win.

I BELIEVE I got more enjoyment from watching Limerick win that All-Ireland than I did when we won in '73. Although maybe I'm doing that a disservice because it was so far back. I obviously got immense enjoyment out of winning the All-Ireland as a player, but I guess everything that had gone on outside of the game, with my son's ill health and passing, had diluted the experience.

This win, however, was just pure, unbridled joy.

After the match we jumped in a taxi and headed to get a train home.

No hanging around.

Limerick was the place to be. We got to Heuston Station and the first person we met was Danny Healy-Rae. He was getting the same train, and it was fair to say he kept a fair few people entertained.

It was quite the scene. People were moving through carriages non-stop, bumping into old friends and seeing who they could find. A few people recognised me and sure that was only more entertainment. I don't think a train journey ever went by as quickly.

Everyone just sang the whole way back to Limerick. Aaron Gillane's grandmother was with us at one stage, and the lads decided to serenade her. Pure magic.

There were people from Cork and Tipperary with us and they all just joined in with the celebrations. For a moment I found my mind wandering, wondering if the rivalry is maybe going out of sport, before deciding that that particular concern could wait for another day.

I guess it was just the whole novelty factor of seeing a Limerick win.

I'm sure if the lads were to win another four or five in the next 10 years, there wouldn't be too many people from other counties looking to join the sing-song.

We got back to Limerick and at that stage we couldn't even get a foot into any of the pubs in the city. The night ended back home in Patrickswell.

The perfect ending to the greatest of days.

The whole village was out.

I saw people singing and dancing that had never watched a hurling match in their lives. I don't remember the place ever feeling so alive.

At the homecoming I was interviewed on RTÉ by Marty Morrissey. It felt like there were 100,000 people in the Gaelic Grounds. I saw the Patrickswell lads, but I didn't really get chatting to them.

I was also very aware that this was their moment, and I didn't want anyone to bring up the '73 win with them.

WHEN WE WERE celebrating the night of our All-Ireland win, one of our selectors, Jackie Power, was talking to me in the hotel.

Mick Mackey was there, and he walked over during the conversation and mentioned a point I had scored from about 60 yards out on the Cusack Stand side.

'Richie…' he said, leaning in, 'I remember scoring a point just like that in 1940.'

Jackie turned around to him.

'Mick… let him have his moment, you had yours.'

THAT'S THE WAY I felt around the 2018 panel.

This was their day, let them soak it all in.

I ended up bumping into the Patrickswell lads a few days later, down the village, and then there was a night in the club where we were all interviewed on RTÉ.

The lads were obviously thrilled with their achievement, but they were still as full of craic as ever. 'You'll have to take a back seat now, Richie,' one of them told me.

It was great to see them so relaxed about the whole thing.

Of course, I knew the three lads very well, and their families. They couldn't be nicer people. There are no egos involved at all. If they are up in the club, they have all the time in the world for all the kids who come up to them. You'd see them out in the field pucking a ball around with young fellas, making their day.

The three of them made huge contributions in 2018.

I saw them all hurling from an early age. Diarmaid Byrnes is an exceptional young man. He's got his head well screwed on. I was up at the national school when the lads brought back the Liam MacCarthy Cup, and the speech he gave to the kids was outstanding.

He looked at the cup, and then stared out at the children.

'I sat where you are now, and I was going down the wrong road!' he told them.

'Instead, I got involved with hurling in the school… and the club.'

He turned and pointed at the Liam MacCarthy Cup.

'That's what I have to show for it.'

He almost had me crying again. You could see in him that it was from the heart. You could feel what the achievement meant to him, vindication for all the hard work and discipline.

Aaron Gillane is another from a big hurling background.

Aaron's father is hugely into hurling in the club. He trained Ardscoil Rís to a few Harty Cups. His mother's brother, Patsy Harte is from Kildimo, the same parish as Kyle Hayes, and he was a great hurler. He never really made the county teams but he was really talented. Aaron's grand-uncle then is married to Barry Magane's sister. There's connections everywhere.

I know everyone has a soft spot for their own club lads, but the three of them really are top class young men. As are most of the county panel, going by my own experiences with them and what I've heard from others. Declan Hannon is as sound a lad as you could meet. Tom Condon too. It's no surprise that Nicky Quaid is a nice lad, as any of the Quaid's I've known have always been lovely people. They are hurling royalty in Limerick. They're from Feohanagh. Four of our original family were born in Feohanagh as well, and Joe Quaid once told me that if the Bennis' had stayed in Feohanagh, they'd have a great team altogether between ourselves and them.

Cian Lynch was always an artist. You would always see him with a hurley in his hand, doing tricks and whatever.

He's always been capable of doing the impossible, which is exactly what he'd be trying to do, and I felt that was holding him back a bit in his development. The current management have helped him focus more on the simple things. The little magic moments are just sprinkled in at different stages, rather than always going for the audacious. He's Ciarán Carey's nephew, so he's of good hurling stock. His father is a proud Tipperary man too. Cian wouldn't have really won much with Patrickswell coming up through the age grades, but his teams were nearly always there or thereabouts. I thought the picture of him hugging his mother, Valerie out on the pitch after the final whistle was just wonderful.

At the end of the day it's all about family.

Cian really came to the fore in 2018. His best position is midfield. Cian needs freedom, and he's a workaholic. You don't really notice it as much on television, but if you watch him live he pops up everywhere. He'd be up around the full-forward line playing a pass one minute, and before you know it he's snuffing out danger in his own half-back line. In midfield he's got the space to pick out a pass too.

He was always this flamboyant, expressive player, but he's grown into a real team man. Kiely has got them all playing as a team, first and foremost.

JOHN KIELY IS a very impressive fella.

He doesn't take over. He stays in the background when he feels that it's necessary. Players aren't the only ones who develop egos, of course, and I was really impressed with the way Kiely handled the All-Ireland win. He's very level-headed, as are the panel. Sure the players were talking about backing up their All-Ireland win the morning after the final.

Obviously, the incident in New York at the end of 2019, which ended with two of the lads being sent home early by the team management, was regrettable. They acted like foolish young men, and John Kiely was dead right to send them home on the next plane. But, we are all foolish young men and women at different times in our lives, and luckily for some of us there were no mobile phones and social media to show up our actions to the whole world.

I'd imagine most counties that had been waiting so long for an All-Ireland would have the mother of all sessions that night of the All-Ireland win, and deservedly so, but half the Limerick lads, even the younger guys on the squad, were up first thing having their recovery dips in the hotel swimming pool.

I know where we were at that time after the '73 win. The level of focus is just on a whole new level to what Limerick had been used to.

Kiely also made sure that the Liam MacCarthy was never brought into a pub, which was a great idea. He practices what he preaches in terms of respect.

He obviously works the team hard, but the way they play shows huge faith in him. I don't ever recall seeing a team with such an appetite for work. You'd be tired watching them. Brian Cody's great Kilkenny teams brought a huge level of intensity, but they played more of a man-to-man game, where the focus was on winning your individual battles.

Kiely's Limerick team work as one.

Everything is done with a team mentality.

They tackle in groups and attack in numbers. Look at the work Kyle Hayes, Gearóid Hegarty and Tom Morrissey did that year. They never stopped running along those middle 60 yards of the pitch. It's just constant work.

I love how Kiely had them working the ball with such speed, right from the full-back line. They fire short passes at a ferocious speed, and still you hardly ever see a man miscontrol the ball. That shows how much the skills have come on, seeing as how so many players struggled with that game under Dónal.

And they're not afraid to give the ball to a man in a better position. There's nobody out there trying to be the hero.

They actually reverted back to that old style early in the 2019 championship, when they lost to Cork at the Gaelic Grounds. Lads were running into trouble and holding onto the ball for too long. I understand the lads had a meeting after that game and said they would get back to what they were good at.

The next day out, against Waterford, it was out of their system and they won by 20 points, although Waterford were just way off the pace that day.

Cian Lynch was actually the worst culprit against Cork, but from the Waterford game he was back to his best, playing the team game, seeing the bigger picture and driving the team on from midfield. That's a sign of really good management. Identifying an issue and eradicating it immediately.

In other ways they remind me of Kilkenny, particularly in their levels of concentration. I think that might be their biggest attribute. You rarely see any of them switch off. I heard Kiely being asked about comparisons to Kilkenny?

'We're not Kilkenny… we're Limerick!' he fired back.

That's the type of thing that supporters, and players, love to hear. We're not trying to be the next this or that.

We're our own men.

THE IMPACT OF of that All-Ireland win in the county was visible immediately. Limerick City is a rugby town. You only have to walk through town any given weekend to see that. When Munster are playing, the place is decked out with red flags and bunting.

When Limerick are playing, you might get a couple of flags up along the bridges, but the council don't put any up in the town itself. That's slowly improving, but there's still a big difference in the way Munster Rugby and Limerick GAA are treated. There isn't a whole lot of hurling in the city, only Na Piarsaigh really.

We had a little event with the cup in the club in Patrickswell, and about 2,000 people showed up. The Limerick players were all happy to mingle with the crowd and chat away to the kids, signing autographs and taking selfies.

The very next week we had new kids coming down to the club looking to play. It was the biggest boost in numbers we had seen in years. We have 20 girls playing under-10 camogie now, and that is purely as a result of Limerick winning the All-Ireland in 2018. The year before, the team had been struggling to piece together a team of 15 players. They're quite a good team too. I'd say the future of camogie in Patrickswell is looking bright.

You also notice people talking about Limerick hurling in a different way, even people who would be causal enough hurling fans. The style of play is always mentioned, as well as the attitude of the players. It is not just about the scores and the hits anymore.

I got the impression that people enjoyed the fact there was no real superstars in the team either. Of course, there were key players in 2018, but there was no one man who the team relied on. It was never down to one individual.

You look at Cork, who have relied so heavily on Patrick Horgan down the years. If he has an off day, they generally end up in trouble. They've often ended up in trouble even if he's shooting the lights out. Even Kilkenny have often needed TJ Reid to dig them out of a hole.

I remember looking at the top scorers in the 2018 championship, and there were only two Limerick players in the top 10.

Aaron Gillane was seventh, Shane Dowling ninth.

That gives you an indication of how much the responsibility of getting scores was spread around the team. One day Gillane is leading the way, the next day it would be someone else. It's very hard for an opposition to stop your key man when they can't figure out who it is.

Some of the 2018 panel also surprised me.

When the two Morrisseys, Dan and Tom, Graeme Mulcahy and Declan Hannon all made the panel, I had my reservations. There were lads who I felt hadn't been hurling well, so if they were deemed good enough to make the cut I thought we must be struggling.

I was happy to see that every one of those lads proved me 100 per cent wrong. They all ended up being in the running for Hurler of the Year. With the two Morrisseys, it seemed as if the bigger the occasion, the better they played. They weren't hurling great in the games leading up to the Munster final, but on the day they both turned it on. Again, that was another sign of great management.

As was the way the bench was managed.

You had lads stuck on the bench who were coming on and regularly making a real difference in games, yet when they didn't get a place in the starting team there wasn't so much as a whisper of discontent. Kiely had them all on board, all moving in the one direction for the greater good.

Kiely also had a great backroom team, which is key to any successful experience. It's never just a one-man show.

Ger Connell, who was the kitman when I was manger, is still there. Ger is an absolute class act. You would never have to even think, let alone worry, about anything that Ger was organising. You always knew it would be done and done well. He would end up looking after warm-up pitches, hotels and all sorts.

By all accounts the Limerick training sessions are as hard as any match now. They've got subs for their training games, which of course is following the Kilkenny model. The stuff we don't see, that's where All-Irelands are really won. Those cold January nights.

That's when you find out who is serious about the thing. The extra sprints after training. The saying no to nights out. Missing events with family and friends because you can't miss training. You don't want to miss training.

All of that is a lot easier when you know every single member of the panel is on board. You can be sure that none of that Limerick group were complaining about training in 2018. They were absolutely living for it.

I HAD THE cup in the house too, about a fortnight after the final. We had a barbecue with about 30 kids in the back garden, all delighted with life.

Though the whole operation has gone a bit secret service now.

The cup was dropped out to us at 4.0 pm, and whisked away at 9.0 am the following morning. By that stage the relief of winning the All-Ireland had worn off, so we were in full-on celebration mode.

We have pictures of that evening up in the house. Every now and then I catch a glance at those pictures when my mind could be on something completely different, and I can't stop the smile from creeping across my face.

It was wonderful to see so many family and friends getting to enjoy the win, seeing the Liam MacCarthy up close and getting to hold it. Then, of course, all they want to do is puck a ball around.

The effect of little things like that does so much for kids.

It makes them see that dreams can be achieved. In a few years… this could be you. That's the real legacy of an All-Ireland win.

It lights the spark in the next generation.

PART TWO

The Craft

THOMAS BENNIS
(Brother and Teammate)

RICHIE HAD A fair bit of divilment in him as a child.

From a very early age he was always mad for doing things, always on the go. We were all a bit like that to be honest. There was a big forest across the road from us and we'd be out playing all the time. Most of the time we were just killing each other pucking a ball around.

It was a very busy house. When we came home from playing matches we would sit around the table and discuss the whole thing, and our mother would be centre-stage of it all. She would want to know everything that was going on, and as we got older then she would keep any cuttings from the paper or anything like that.

There would be war in the house then if any of us touched them because she wouldn't want them getting damaged or going missing.

WE WERE VERY close growing up, Richie and myself, as there was only a couple of years between us. We did an awful lot of stuff together, and we still do to this day. He's always been a very confident man, and no matter what you want to get done, he'll get it done. His choice of language might not always be the best, but you always knew where you stood with him.

Patrickswell was a great place to be a child at the time. We couldn't wait to get home from school every day so we could get out and play. Even on Christmas Day a crowd of us used to go down and play soccer in the field for about two hours.

We did that every year.

Our childhood was all about activity, as we didn't really have much else, and Richie would be at the centre of things. When I think of Richie as a kid, it's just hurling, hurling… hurling.

Richie always had a talent for hurling, but we really started to notice it when he was playing minor. By that stage he was able to do things with a ball that most of us couldn't. He had fierce skill to his game.

He might not have been the fastest fella around, but he had everything else. You always felt very secure with him on your team. He knew he had the skill too. He wouldn't be satisfied with beating a fella once; Richie would want to beat him two or three times. He had huge confidence in himself, and he had a bit of the showboat about him.

There was a particular referee we used to have quite often, and whenever he gave Richie a free, Richie would move the ball forward two or three feet.

The referee would move it back but Richie would keep trying to inch it forward. He would always have run-ins with that ref, but it didn't stop him trying his luck.

It drove the poor referee mad.

But he worked hard on his hurling. At the same time you could see that he had bags of a natural talent. He played full-back for Patrickswell in the mid-60s, when I was half-back, and even though he was only 19 or 20 he would be telling lads what to do and where to go, all that kind of thing, and he was a commanding presence even at that stage. He had fierce confidence in himself.

Once he got to minor level, and started to realise his talent, you could see that playing for Limerick was at the forefront of his thoughts. He had such natural control of the ball. He could balance a ball on his hurley and run the length of the field, no bother.

He had fierce wit on the field as well.

I remember we were playing a county championship match one year, and we were winning by 10 or 11 points with the match nearly over. They won a free and one of their players was trying to rise the ball and hit it, but was struggling.

Next thing Richie shouts over to him, 'Hold on a minute, and I'll go get you a shovel'. That's the type of man he was.

He was great craic, but if you didn't know him, you'd kill him.

« CHAPTER 5 »

I AM A Patrickswell man. My whole life has been spent in the Patrickswell area, but the story as to how we arrived here is far from straightforward.

It begins in a timber barn in Dromcollogher in September, 1926.

The barn was being used as a temporary cinema, and would also hold other events such as dances and charity nights. One night, during a film screening, the barn caught fire. Cinemas were closed in Cork on Sundays, and so one entrepreneurial individual, who worked in one of those Cork cinemas, had taken the liberty of 'borrowing' films from his place of employment.

He would travel around and lend the films for screenings in nearby parishes. Of course, this was not exactly legal. On this particular night in Dromcollogher, a bunch of locals left Sunday evening mass and made their way to a loft in the barn for a screening of a film called *Ten Commandments*.

During the screening, a candle fell onto the film; it caught fire and the blaze spread so quickly that the building was almost immediately engulfed in flames.

People panicked.

Some jumped from the loft, a drop of about eight feet.

Others tried to climb out windows at the back of the barn. Some escaped, many others were trapped. Forty-eight people were killed. The incident became known as The Dromcollogher Burning, and it was Ireland's worst fire disaster until the Whiddy Island disaster in 1979 and The Stardust fire in 1981. All but one of the people who died that night are buried in a large grave at the church.

My father, Garret Bennis was fortunate not to be in the ground with them. He was inside when the barn caught fire. His understanding was that a sergeant outside the barn told people to relax, and they would get the fire extinguished.

So a large group of people waited inside, terrified, thinking the fire would soon be under control. However, the fire brigade seemed to run out of water, or at least that was the message that spread inside the barn. That led to further panic.

There was a mad rush for the door.

Dad was around 26 at the time, and would have been light and slender enough. He managed to help a few people escape before squeezing himself out a narrow window. He fell down onto a railing and needed 12 stitches, but he survived.

A CLOUD HUNG over the place, and all involved, for quite some time. Apparently, some people who were there that night and witnessed the tragedy wore black for the rest of their lives.

Eventually life moved on.

Dad met and married my mother, May Delacey who came from a small town between Newcastle West and Dromcollogher. By 1935 they had five children, but were living with my mother's parents, which was fairly common practice then.

My father heard that there were jobs going at Shannon Airport, with a company who were building runways. So he decided to head on down and look for work. By bicycle, the journey from Dromcollogher to Shannon was a good 70 kilometres. Each way.

He got the job, but still had no house for his five children.

There was a possibility that he would have to try to get a house near the airport, which would have meant I would have ended up playing for Clare. Thank God he called into Riordans' pub in Patrickswell for a drink on the way home.

He wasn't really a drinking man, but this was a special occasion. He ordered himself a bottle of stout and got talking to whoever was sitting around the bar. He explained about the job in Shannon, and not having a house, and some fella at the bar told him about a house nearby which had just become available.

He didn't think about it too much. Houses like that were generally already lined up for a family member or a friend. Anyway, he headed off down the road home shortly after and bumped into a buddy of his, who told him the same story about this house, and that they were looking for someone to take it.

Dad cycled on up the road to meet the owner, who decided that Garret Bennis fitted the bill. Just like that, the Bennis family were on the move, and the Clare dilemma had been avoided.

Dad ended up getting a job on a nearby farm, and lived in that house from 1935 until he died in 1964.

In total, my parents had 13 children.

Six boys and seven girls, nice and even. I believe they lost a child as well, early enough in their marriage. This is probably a good time to make yourself a cup of tea!

MY SISTER, MAISIE died in 2015, in her late eighties. She had 26 grandchildren, and 17 great-grandchildren when she passed away.

She married a lovely man by the name of Thomas Fortune. Unfortunately, Thomas died young following an accident working in a sandpit, which caved in on top of him. He survived but his health was ruined and he only lived a few years after it, dying in his forties.

Maisie was left with nine children, the oldest 14 years-old and the youngest just 12 months. There was no dole or social welfare to help the family, and Maisie had to work two and three jobs to survive, but every one of those kids turned out brilliantly. Maisie was a wonderful lady.

And the rest of my sisters and brothers?

CATHY MOVED TO England when she was 17. Her boyfriend moved

with her, to Leamington Spa, and they got married over there. My mother was the only person in our family who went to the wedding, because that was all we could afford. I don't think my father would have been able for a trip like that anyway.

Sean was next, the first boy. He left Patrickswell to hurl with the other half of the parish, who were naturally our biggest rivals. He had married down there, and that influenced him.

Then there was Gerald, a former chairman of the Limerick county board. He worked in the post office and married a lady by the name of Nora Shinners. She was secretary to the Mayor of Limerick at the time, and was big into politics.

Pat worked in the post office with Gerald, and moved to Dublin to work in the Department of Education. He married a lady from Dooradoyle, and his son, Eoghan Bennis played football for Dublin in the early 2000s. He was good too, but I think soccer was his first love. He was playing with UCD and they were able to offer some money towards the mortgage.

Angela worked in Woolworths in Limerick, and she married Patrick Kirby. They are parents of Gary Kirby. Angela is like a mother to us all, constantly watching out for everyone; and always there when we need her.

Phil was a machinist, and he married in Patrickswell. He managed the club to win 12 county championships, and also Limerick to a league title as well as Minor and under-21 All-Irelands.

Peggy married a chap named Michael Hackett from Newcastle West, and they lived in Shannon all their lives. He died young from a brain haemorrhage but she's still out there.

Next was Thomas, who only lives up the road from me. He was a prominent Limerick referee for a number of years. Then I came along.

I was followed by Eileen, who is married and living in Mungret, not too far away from me. She spent a number of years in Africa.

Peter, my brother and neighbour, was my youngest brother. He also played for Limerick, and he sadly passed away from a heart attack in 2016.

Joan is the baby of the family, or as she calls herself, the rinsing of the teapot. She married a fella named Jackie Gorman, who hurled for Clare. We had a fair few confrontations down the years.

MY FIRST MEMORY of the house in Patrickswell was when I was five.

At that time, there was no washing machines or anything like that, just a big bath of water in the middle of the floor. I hated Mondays, because that was the day my mother would wash all the clothes.

The whole house would smell of the washing for hours.

So you had this bath of boiling hot water in front of a huge open fire, about eight foot wide. We were running around the kitchen blackguarding one day and I ended up getting pushed into the bath.

The water was so hot that I was burned all over my back. A friend of the family, who would often call into the house, happened to be passing by and he was able to pull me out of the water. I was in so much pain that I couldn't even be moved to hospital.

It was probably one of those things that would be dealt with much more effectively nowadays. I ended up having to spend three months confined to bed, with a nurse cycling out from Adare every day to change the dressings. Seemingly it was touch and go for a long time.

The fella who pulled me out was full of divilment himself, and years later he would joke that he should have left me in the bath.

I'm sure you can imagine the scene in that house with so many of us. There was messing all the time. My father worked six days a week. On Sundays he would go up to the farm and they would supply the milk for the house. That was one of the big perks for the family.

As well as paying his wages, the farm gave my father plenty of vegetables. We always had potatoes, turnips and cabbage. We'd get as much milk as we wanted, and firewood.

That haul provided us with enough to live on.

We always had two pigs up the back of the house ourselves, so my mother was always kept busy.

She was supposed to head off to South Africa to work as a trainee nurse but her sister ended up going instead of her, and so she stayed at home to mind her parents. She was before her time, very intelligent without being educated. She was always reading.

Generally, there wouldn't really be more than 10 of us in the house. There were two or three beds in each room. They were big rooms, one for the boys and one for the girls. One had been built on before we moved in, which we christened the new room.

We loved the old room because it was at the back of the fire, so it was roasting. The new room was much colder, but there would usually be enough of us in there to warm each other up. They gave the girls the new room because it was more modern.

We were happy enough, because we knew that we had really got the better deal. Not that you would admit it.

I'm not sure what growing up in such a small house does to a person, but I do know that that house is the reason I still can't stomach the sight of porridge. We had it for breakfast every morning.

One time, I got the measles. The cure was to be left in bed in a dark room. Sleep it off, more or less. The porridge would be brought in, someone would be messing and it would get spilled and I'd be left lying there with the smell of it, not able to do anything about it.

I haven't eaten it since the day I moved out of that house.

Mary, my good wife, tries to get me to eat it every now and then, but she hasn't succeeded yet and it's a battle she's not likely to win anytime soon.

WE HURLED OUT the front, against the wall of the house, or in the bit of woodland beside us where two big trees acted as goalposts. There would be five or six of us out hurling at the wall any evening.

Our next door neighbour, John Lynch was a fine hurler too. He was an only child, so he practically became part of our family. He would always call down to us, and if anything was happening, he'd be part of it.

We'd stay up playing cards, dancing or playing rings. If we were heading up to the shop we'd call in to Ms Lynch to see if she needed anything. Her mother-in-law was staying in the house and would call us in to her little room and hand us an envelope to send off to her daughter, which had her pension in it.

It would have been about two pounds.

We hadn't been a hurling family. But since there were so many of us and not a whole lot else to do, hurling quickly became our pastime of choice.

Getting your hands on a hurley was an adventure in itself.

« CHAPTER 6 »

A GROUP OF us would head up to watch a match in Patrickswell, and without fail, there would always be about half a dozen hurleys broken during the game.

The trick was to race out onto the field to grab whatever bits of shrapnel you could get a hand to, then you would take it home and mend it as best you could to fashion your own hurley. I think it was Gerald and Phil who came up with the idea, but I soon showed a natural talent for procuring hurleys.

Other local kids saw what we were up to and caught on.

There would be a queue along the sideline of lads waiting for a chance to dart out for a broken hurley because we were all in the same boat. The trick was to know where to stand, and more importantly, who to trip.

There was no teams for under-12 or under-13 at the time, so the first match I played in was at under-16, even though I would only have been about 10 or 11. The good thing was that you would always have two or three from the family on the one team, because that team would be covering ages from 10 up to 14 for the Bennis household.

I was always put in the forwards with Peter.

Thomas would have been in the backs, and the three of us always played in the same teams together at underage level.

When we were playing out in the woods we would always put one of the girls in goals, which, you can imagine, didn't go down well. Angela seemed to end up in there the most. The thing was, she was a good hurler herself, so she would be dying to be out pucking around instead of standing in the goals.

Peggy was a good hurler too. On the occasions that they weren't in goal the boys wouldn't go any easier on them, which is just the way the girls would have wanted it.

WE WERE ALLOWED to walk to school. On a fine day we could cut across the field, but on wet days we had to take a longer route along the road, about a two and a half mile trek. There would be a gang of about 10 or 12 of us walking the same route; we'd end up meeting more along the way. A lot of them had to walk farther that us.

Early rises weren't a problem in our house.

We would all be jumping out of bed to get some hurling in before the long walk to school. A big gang of us out pucking around right up to the very last minute, that dashing off up the road so we weren't late.

There were 68 children in the school, and I know that because you had to have that number to have three teachers working there. If you dipped below 68, the school was reduced to two teachers.

I don't know how they did it, but one way or another they were able to make sure there was always 68 pupils. They would always be able to find a name somewhere.

All 13 of us went to that school. You had another big family down the road, the Toomeys and there was about 15 of them. The Coughlans were a big family too. It was a big breeding area, I guess. Those three families alone would nearly have kept the school going. As one child from a family was leaving the school they would have another getting ready to start there.

A good, consistent production line.

There were two classrooms. One big classroom had all of fifth and sixth classes, then the other room had a big curtain drawn across to divide it into two.

Infants, first and second classes were on one side.

Third and fourth classes on the other.

It was mayhem, but I'm sure it was probably the same everywhere. There was no school in the village of Patrickswell, so we were a bit further down the road but still in the parish itself. The teacher who taught me for my Communion actually taught my daughter her Communion too.

I didn't mind school so much, but it would be a stretch to say that I liked it. School itself was fine, but the homework was a different story. I thought I should be outside hurling, not stuck in the house with my head in a book. You had to do a primary exam at that time, and that decided what class you would be going to in secondary school.

We had one teacher who wasn't too fond of Irish, so he'd dedicate all the time to maths, or 'sums' as he called it. He thought we were all flying it, but we were all just copying each other behind his back. He was convinced that he was this brilliant maths teacher, leading this young group of high performers.

He ended up moving on a few months before we were meant to sit the primary exam, so this new fella, Mr Garvey arrived in from town to take the class.

He was a lovely man, but he had a problem on his hands. It was four months before our primary, and he could see that we hadn't a hope of passing Irish. The Irish exam was basically a composition, so his bright idea was to pick three from the list of possibilities, get us to learn them off by heart, and pray that one of the three came up.

We obliged, and to our amazement one of them came up. We all got higher marks for Irish than we did for anything else.

We liked Garvey.

He brought some hurling with him, and asked the farmer next door if we could use the field to play. You couldn't really call it training, we just pucked a ball around. We generally only had one sliothar anyway. We had a lot of good hurlers. I remember he organised a match against the nearest school, my first local derby, and we beat them.

With so many of us packed into the building, there was rarely a dull moment at school.

You'd be guaranteed a row at lunchtime.

There were two parts to the parish, the Ballybrown side and the Patrickswell side. In the mornings, crowds from the two parts would often bump into each other and that's normally how the row would start.

Then, naturally, you'd have to have another row on the way home with the same fella you had fought earlier. The red pump was our local landmark, situated at a little junction outside a house where the two crowds would meet.

You had a crowd that would be heading towards Ballyhanrahan, to the south of Patrickswell, and we'd be heading in the other direction towards the village. We would meet at the red pump.

And, without fail, there would always be some action.

I WAS NEVER likely to go down the road before the Kerry footballer, Paul Galvin and pursue a life in fashion. As you could imagine, there was no such thing as walk-in wardrobes, at least not in our little part of the world.

There was no such thing as a school uniform.

We all had a big raincoat and you had to mind it with your life.

We dressed up in suits going to mass on Sundays, but we would struggle out of them the minute we got home. I normally wore a little corduroy jacket with a zip up the front. It was the same clothes every day, more or less.

I remember for Sean's wedding I got a suit, and I cried because Thomas got long pants but my mother got me short pants. That was probably the first time I ever really expressed any interest in what I was wearing.

I was in the damned short pants until I was around 12.

My father would mend all of our shoes too. He'd buy a big wedge of leather, and fix the soles whenever it was needed. He was very handy. He'd be quiet enough, just tipping away at whatever needed to be done.

I have great memories of growing up. People look back at that time and say you had nothing, but we had everything really.

We had company, we had enough to eat and we had clean clothes.

Our mother was strict on the cleanliness front, and we had to wash ourselves every evening. We had no running water, so we would head out to a barrel or whatever was around and wash ourselves before bed.

She used to say that although you might have a hole in your pants, it would be a clean hole. She would have made a brilliant Minister for Finance.

Money was obviously very sparse with 13 of us, but she managed to get a new suit for every one of us, tailor made, for Communion and Confirmation. Confirmation was only held every three years, so we would end up having three for Confirmation and one for Communion, leaving my mother with four children to dress every three years at least.

How she used to manage was down to the two pigs we had.

We'd buy them about three times a year, rear them and then sell them on. She ran an account with a shop on Willian Street in Limerick City, called Meades, which was run by a gentleman by the name of Fitzgibbon. He would give her credit on the condition that when she would get the cheque from selling the pigs, she would bring it in to him.

Sure enough, the minute she got the cheque she would head off into Meades, and that covered all the clothes she needed to buy.

« CHAPTER 7 »

LIKE EVERY FAMILY around us, religion was a big presence in our lives. We said our prayers in the morning and every night. Get up in the morning, say our prayers, out for a quick bit of hurling, and then run off to school.

It was a good old routine.

We ate healthy, the house was spotlessly clean and we were always outside. When summer rolled around there would always be work laid on for us. By us, I mean Thomas, Peter and myself generally, because the rest of the lads had their own jobs at that stage. It was things like thinning turnips or sugar beet.

There would be a row of turnip seed, and when they grew to a certain height they would need to be thinned down, leaving a bit of room about every 10 inches for the turnip to expand and grow properly. We would spend the days in these huge, sprawling fields, down on our knees the whole time.

We tied coarse bags around our knees to stop them getting badly grazed. Depending on the farm, they might give you something to eat, but we often had to fall on our back-up, which was a cold bottle of tea and a few slices of bread.

It was tough enough work, and you wouldn't exactly be looking forward to it, but it was just part of paying the bills. We'd make about £100 during the holidays, working away for around a month, and then we would get three or four weeks when we were as free as birds.

The real incentive was the reward you got from home, because for doing all that work over the summer our mother would take us out for a day in town a few months later. It was the best day of the year. We would walk up to get the 12 o'clock bus, and we always made sure that our mother had us up there in plenty of time for fear of missing it.

WHEN WE GOT to Limerick, we would stock up on sweets in Woolworths and then get fish and chips in the Capri, right in the middle of O'Connell Street.

It was the only day of the year we would be in town, so in our eyes it made all of that hard work worth it. We'd actually be in Dublin more than Limerick, because we would go up to visit Maisie, once she was living there.

It was normally December 8 when we went in to Limerick – the farmers day – so town would be thronged. It was a bit of an assault on the senses, and we would bump into loads of kids we knew, all in the same situation.

All of us talking about the same thing, mad for the fish and chips in the Capri.

We nearly always did the shopping on a Friday night. Since we were getting milk and all our vegetables from the farm we only needed to get the same three items every week.

Twelve pounds of butter.

A stone of sugar.

And a big bag of tea.

We cycled down, stocked up and cycled back. We had about 12 bikes at the house and, basically, it was whoever was first up got the best bike.

We'd cycle up to Dromcollagher, which was a good 20 miles away. The roads were in bad condition, as were the bikes but, even though we were all skin and bone. we had no problem with fitness.

My father would have picked up the bikes from different places and then mend them for us. Most nights he would have a bike turned upside down in the kitchen, mending a puncture or fixing a chain. He was brilliant at that.

WE ALWAYS HAD meat for dinner, either bacon or pig's head.

Fish was on Fridays.

And we always had a roast dinner every Sunday. A fella by the name of Finbarr Martell would drive around on Thursday evenings delivering the fish, and our house would be last on his list because he would stay there for hours. He was big into his hurling, and would play rings, cards and whatever else we had around the place.

At the end of the evening, he would leave a big fish for the dinner the next day. When we sat down for our Friday feast of fish, all cramped into this tiny little house together, we all thought we were in heaven.

OUR HOUSE WAS located at the front of a small road that led up to a big house called Newbarragh House. A man named Jack Smith lived there alone.

He had a housemaid and there were always about eight or nine additional staff working around the house. The staff would stay in rooms in the cellar, and there was a bell outside each of those rooms that you could ring if you needed someone for some work.

Jack was a sort of gentleman farmer.

He never did any work himself, but he was always dressed up and would look the part. He used to drive around in this green van during the day, and then on Sundays he would head off to church in a fabulous Jaguar. He only ever drove that on Sundays, save for the odd time he was heading off to some mart.

The very minute he was out the gate, we would all dash up to his house and sneak into the orchard, and grab as many pears as we could pocket. And whatever else we could manage. He knew what we were up to, of course, but never said a word.

I'm sure he would have just given us the pears if we had been kind enough to ask him, but that wouldn't have been half as enjoyable.

My father worked for Jack for many years, and then the Dillion family bought the place around 1960. They are still there now.

We lived in our little lodge from 1935 until 1960, before moving down the road. One of the perks at the time was that if you were long enough working for a farmer you were entitled to an acre and the council would build a house on it.

We were lucky. I think they gave us quite a big acre. The new house felt very modern to us, with new luxuries like running water. We didn't know ourselves.

I still remember the move quite clearly.

We brought all our stuff down on a horse and float. It was massive exciting, and felt like a real adventure. It also meant we were nearer school, which is generally not high on most kids' list of priorities, but for us that meant more time to hurl in the mornings.

There were three rooms. At that stage Seán was married, so there was only about eight of us left in the house. My mother was minding her own father, so he had joined the crew.

One of the big advantages of the new house was that we had a full field for hurling. To us it was Croke Park.

Or more likely, the Gaelic Grounds.

MY FIRST TIME in the Gaelic Grounds was 1955, when a group of us cycled in to the city to see the Munster final. I would have been about 10 years old.

Limerick were playing Clare, and won, even though Clare had been out-and-out favourites. They had beaten Tipperary already, while Limerick had come past Waterford. I don't remember the occasion all that clearly, but I do remember watching Dermot Kelly. He was centre-forward for Limerick, and was being marked by Clare's top player, Dan McInerney.

Kelly beat the daylights out of him and scored 1-12.

The first time I properly remember going to the stadium was 1961, to watch Cork play Tipperary. We cycled up again, and parked up the bikes outside the ground.

We would always be there in plenty of time, so the problem was you would be waiting for ages after the match to get at your bike because there would be so many more on top of it.

They said the official attendance on the day was around 61,000 but they reckoned a lot more than that managed to squeeze in and it was reported they turned away another 10,000 people. You could barely move inside, and it was a roasting hot day.

They were selling bottles of water for a shilling, and they ran out of minerals fairly quickly. We, like many others in the ground, were there to see Christy Ring.

He was an absolute idol to us. I used to travel around to see a good few county finals with a friend of mine, Davy Moran. In Cork you would get crowds of 30,000 people at a county final, most of them there to catch a glimpse of Ring in action.

He was a mythical figure.

In 1956 a bunch of us had gone up the road to listen to the All-Ireland final at Jack Sullivan's house because he had a battery radio. Wexford beat Cork, but Ring scored 1-5. As the match was winding down the battery started to go on the radio, so we were all squashing up closer to hear the action.

We had been at the Munster final in 1956 to see Limerick play Cork. A bus conductor whom we knew was marking Ring, and had told us his one ambition was to hold him scoreless. Limerick were about five or six points ahead and Ring hadn't scored a single point. Cork moved him further out the field. Our bus conductor pal wanted to follow up, but Mick Mackey, who was over the team at the time, told him to stay inside.

Ring ended up scoring two goals.

Cork won.

I would go to the Gaelic Grounds at every available opportunity. In 1958 I was a substitute on the minor team in the city final. I was only about 12 at the time. Phil was on the team, as were Tony Boyd and Eamon Carey, all great hurlers. We were playing St Patrick's, who were the dominant force in underage hurling in Limerick. I got my first ever pair of boots for that match.

There was a farmer up the road who had an acre of turnips which needed to be thinned, and he was a bit behind schedule. His problem arrived at just the right time for me. A pair of boots cost around one pound and 19 shillings.

My mother couldn't afford that. But I knew that we already had our summer turnip target met for the family. A deal was struck. I got the acre done in around four days. I got three pounds for the four days of work.

It was a good rate.

My father would get around three pound and 15 shillings for a week's work. I gave a pound to my mother and went off to buy the boots in Nestors in town. It was the only sports shop in the city. I was delighted with my new boots, with four big studs at the front and two at the back.

On the day of the game, I was an unused substitute.

The boots never even made it past the bench.

MY FATHER WAS a lovely, quiet man.

A gentle man. If you misbehaved he would just have a quiet word with you and that would be enough to make you check yourself.

My mother had a different approach. She would kind of shout at you, and still you might take no notice of it. They were two very different types of disciplinarians.

My mother was big into Irish music. We had our own gramophone in the house, which was still a bit of a novelty. We had a constant supply of music. Nearly every week, either someone from our own family or one of the neighbours would head off into town and come back with a record. Then everyone would be around in ours that evening, dancing and celebrating the best of life

We would be in bed listening.

Trying to figure out whether they were doing half-steps, waltzes or foxtrots? My mother would happily teach all the neighbours the different dances. Generally, one of us would get to stay up and control the gramophone, which was a real treat.

You got to sit there, wind the gramophone up, change the needle for every record, and just watch all these people dancing away. I was fascinated by music, and got a real thrill out of watching someone play an instrument or getting to hear a new record.

The main music event locally was on Sundays in a large field half way between Patrickswell and Adare. They would set up a platform, which was basically a large timber floor in a field. One of the local fellas would then play the accordion, and you would have upwards of 100 people dancing away all night.

The next morning the floor would be taken up and packed away for the following week. The Parish Priest down in Adare was very strict, and he'd always be there to make sure there were no shenanigans going on, batting at hedges to make sure nobody was stealing a moment of romance away from the dancefloor.

As my mother loved dancing, she would head down every Sunday. Out of the 13 of us, not one of us could sing, but we all loved the dancefloor.

Those dances were mad craic. Timing was very important though, and not just when you were in the middle of a waltz. At that time there were more Protestants in Adare than there were Catholics.

There would be hymns in the nearby Presbyterian church at 6.0 pm, so most people would go along to that first. I always felt like people were trying to fit in something respectable before the madness of the dance that night.

WE WERE OUTSIDE at every given opportunity. When we started going to hurling training, it just put a tiny bit of structure on what we had been doing every night anyway.

Hurling training in Patrickswell was not very official.

Every single night whoever was around would head down to the club and we'd spend three hours killing each other. If it was bright enough when we'd get home afterwards, we'd spend another hour pucking against a wall.

We had to be accurate off the wall, especially when we lived in the lodge, because if we fired the ball over it someone had to traipse off into the woods to try find it.

And you had to find it.

We only had one ball.

I absolutely loved playing hurling from the very first time I pucked a ball around. I felt immediately drawn to it. All I wanted to do was have a hurl in my hand. It was the only thing I knew really.

They were great days, but life moved along faster, and faster still, in my teenage years.

I was 18 when my father died. He had gone up to work for Lord Harrington, because he had always been very good with horses. We're not sure, but we think he got the drag off a horse and it strained his heart. He went in for a check-up one day and I remember thinking he looked really well when he came home.

He had always been a fine looking man, and always dressed well. That evening he was getting my brothers out of the car, and he just started crying softly.

I realised then that he felt his time was up.

TB was rampant at the time.

Two of my sisters got it. Initially that's what they thought my father had. They thought I potentially had it too at one stage. I had been called back for a second x-ray, but it was a false alarm, thank God.

The cure for TB, or treatment to be more accurate, was six months in bed, with all the windows open.

My father was treated for TB, but that wasn't his problem at all. He ended up getting pneumonia from lying around in the cold for so long. When they realised it wasn't TB, it was already too late. He was moved back to the Regional Hospital and died of a heart complaint at 64.

It was a tough time for the family. Most especially my sister Maisie who ended up burying her husband and father within 12 months of each other.

Both young men.

THE LOSS OF my father left a huge hole in the family.

Everyone ended up taking on different bits around the house.

I took over the garden, and while I was good at planting and looking after the crops I didn't really know the value of everything.

I wanted to grow some lettuce, so one day I went off and bought six pence worth of lettuce seed. It didn't look like much, but I thought it would probably be enough for what I needed. Anyway, I could always come back and pick up some more seed, if I needed to?

I soon learned that six pence worth of lettuce seed was enough to sow an area twice the size of the house.

Before I knew it, I had lettuce everywhere.

The family started finding stashes of lettuce turning up in the most unlikely places around the house. One day a lady named Ms Fitzgibbon called out to see my mother. She was the head lady in a canteen at a factory that employed 500 people. She saw all the lettuce peaking out of every corner of the house and asked if we were selling it?

I gave her a good deal, filled a few bags and she ended up calling out a few more times for a restock. I made 30 pounds, and very nearly went into the lettuce business. That six pence worth of seed is still probably the best investment I ever made.

I'm sure my father would have been proud of the books after that bit of business.

PART THREE

Limerick Roads

TIMMY O'NEILL
(Patrickswell teammate and trainer,
and Patrickswell historian)

LIKE RICHIE, I'M Patrickswell born and bred, so he would have been an idol to all of us because he was one of the first Patrickswell men to wear the county jersey.

Even when he was playing minor or under-21, he was kind of a star.

When we won our first county championship I was only 13, so you can imagine what it was like for me to be watching these lads bring the cup back. Today they just bring it to schools, but Patrickswell was such a tidy little village at the time that the captain of the team and a few other players brought the cup around to every single house.

I can still remember the sight of the cup full of whiskey and all that. We lived right in the heart of the village and it was great excitement.

When we were growing up we looked up to the hurlers big time, because it was the only game played really. If you had a county medal or even played in a senior county final, that gave you status.

Richie always had a little bit more than most because of his exploits on the field, as well as his personality, which was always brash and loud. But it was never in an arrogant way. He was a very outgoing guy.

We used to see them playing backs and forwards in training. They might only have 18 players on the panel, so the only way that they could play a match would be to play six backs and six forwards, with the centrefield lads hitting in the ball, and you could see Richie doing 90 per cent of the shouting.

What you see with Richie is what you get, and that's always been the case as far as I've known him.

I ENDED UP hurling with Richie in Patrickswell, and then I actually ended up training him. I would have been a selector with him too later on, so our paths crossed in lots of ways.

His confidence was always striking.

When I used to watch Ronan O'Gara playing for Munster or Ireland, and how confident he had to be over kicks, it always reminded me of Richie.

If O'Gara missed a kick, that was it, and he would just focus again on the next one. He wouldn't be apologising for missing one or feeling sorry for himself. Richie had the same mentality.

When Richie was taking frees, if it went over the bar he was the star, but if it didn't go over he wouldn't take any shit from anybody. If someone said, 'How did you miss that?', Richie would point out the other nine he had put over.

He always seemed to be impervious to nerves or criticism. He didn't give a damn, or at least that was the impression we got.

Even though I was that bit younger, he was very approachable as a teammate. He was also very supportive of lads who wouldn't have been as skilled as him. With the club teams there was obviously more of a mixture when it came to talent, whereas with the county everyone was at a certain level.

But he was always quite tolerant of people. In a lot of cases, if you were a less skilful hurler, getting the ball to Richie was usually one of your go-to exit strategies. With Patrickswell, Richie turning up in the No. 11 jersey would be enough to intimidate some opponents.

I'm sure he wouldn't say this himself, but while he was well-known for his frees and his scoring, and although we had some great county players – guys like Seán Foley, Phil Bennis, Tony O'Brien etc – Richie was one of the best hurlers in the 1960s and '70s under a dropping ball.

He never pulled back, and he never minded the centre-back pulling on him. He had a great way of protecting himself with the hurley while keeping the other hand free. I always saw that as one of his signature skills.

That tolerance he had for others was also noticeable when I started training Patrickswell. I was not a good hurler. I won underage county championships but I never could get on the senior team, so the only way I could become involved was the fact that I was handy at the training.

I picked a lot of brains in the '70s about physical training and that sort of thing.

I trained an under-21 team in 1975 and '76 and then I was asked to train the senior team. I felt a little bit like, 'God, I'm going to be training Richie and Phil, Seán Foley, these kind of guys', but they were all great and very cooperative.

Richie's attitude was 'OK, he knows his stuff about training so we'll do what he says', even though I didn't have the talent he had and was younger than him. There was no change in our relationship when I became trainer. That said, you wouldn't want to be sensitive around him.

He says what he thinks, even if it isn't right or it isn't couched in a particular way. I remember just going with the flow a few times, and then at a quieter time saying, 'Look, you were out of order there', and he'd accept that. He was very easy to work with as a player.

HE'S ALWAYS REMAINED a big presence around the club, even after he stopped playing. As recently as 2013-14, I had moved back to Patrickswell after living in Dublin for a while, and I got involved with the senior team again.

I was kind of just asked to help out a bit, and Richie was a selector. I must say that those nights at training were great, just talking with him and hearing all the old stories.

He's didn't always have it easy when he was playing, and we would have known that at the time, but Richie always gave his hurling his all.

« CHAPTER 8 »

PATRICKSWELL IS ONE of those small Irish villages that has made quite a mark considering its size, at least in terms of sport. For those of you unfamiliar with the village, it sits about a 10 minute drive from Limerick City.

Our house then is another short drive away from the centre of the village.

The first thing you'd probably notice if you approached the village from the city side is the small pump on the right hand side of the road, just as you come into the place. That's a holy well, which is said to have been visited by St Patrick himself. Hence the name of the village. A small walk down the road brings you to the club.

Patrickswell GAA Club.

If the saint gave us our name, the club made it.

LIKE SO MANY clubs in rural Ireland, Patrickswell has endured plenty of ups and downs. The club colours are blue and gold – the same colours as Tipperary – which is a nod to the uncertainty that surrounded the club previously.

Having been formed in the 1930s, the club struggled to sustain itself in the early years. A lack of playing numbers forced the club to break up for five or six years, before reforming in the mid-1940s.

Tom Ryan's father, Willie was one of the founding members. He came from Clonoulty in Tipperary, which is how we ended up wearing the famous blue and gold. Funnily enough, the years when the club was lying dormant went a long way to cementing one of the most consistent features in the life of any Patrickswell hurler... our rivalry with Ballybrown. Geography dictated that there would always have been a rivalry there anyway, given the fact the two parishes are neighbours, but the events surrounding Patrickswell's disbandment and reformation ensured the relationship between the two would always have that extra bit of bite.

When there was no club in Patrickswell, a bunch of lads that still wanted to play hurling ended up togging out for Ballybrown. When Patrickswell reformed a bunch of those same lads came back to hurl for their home club, which in turn left Ballybrown without some of their best players.

Since then it's always been a fiercely intense rivalry.

I couldn't tell you how many matches between the two clubs didn't even get finished.

That rivalry is still going strong to this day, thankfully. The GAA needs those rivalries to keep the sport alive. If we were to ever lose those local rivalries, then I think we'd be finished. Of course, it's not as serious now as it was during my playing days.

You have lads from rival clubs out socialising together now, and even hanging out together the night before a match. I'm not saying there is anything wrong with that, but it naturally removes some of the bite in those games. If we were caught doing that, I'd imagine we would have been dropped. If not excommunicated.

IT DIDN'T TAKE long to get a taste for success with the club.

I played up through the underage teams, and we won our first junior county title in 1955, beating Pallasgreen, 4-2 to 2-6. There were great celebrations after.

Lemonade and ice-cream all-round.

At that age you think that this will just be the way it always is, but the reality is often much harsher. The following year, we went from winning medals to not even being able to put together a team to play senior hurling. It was a problem that is still all too familiar for rural GAA clubs in every pocket of the country.

We were back playing at junior level in 1957, and won the county title again, but that was followed by another lean period. Seven of our 1957 team emigrated to London in search of work. Losing seven players leaves a massive hole in a small community. It's even worse when they happen to be seven of your best hurlers.

It took the club a while to recover.

Eventually, a bunch of new families moved into the area and that helped to pad out the teams again. Between our own family, the Careys and the Caseys alone, there was the guts of a good team. We managed to compete well over the next few years.

There were some teams we played against where you meet the same old faces again and again. Other teams would be made up from a completely different bunch of lads within a few months. We lost a county semi-final in 1961 to Western Gaels, who were a selection of all the junior teams in West Limerick.

Imagine playing the Harlem Globetrotters, if the Harlem Globetrotters were made up of junior hurlers from the West Limerick countryside? They scraped past us by a few points, but we made them work for it.

Around the same time. I was playing a bit of hurling for the Tech in the city, along with my brother, Thomas. We ended up winning an All-Ireland with them. It was quite the achievement, given the fact that they had no interest at all in hurling before we came along.

There was a decent group of us who wanted to play.

We felt we had the numbers and the players to put a serious side together. Besides ourselves, there were three Tipperary minors, a Clare minor and a few other solid players. We went up to the army field around the back of the school and organised some training.

We were there one night and saw a fella we knew named Tony Wall, who was in the army, and we asked him if he fancied training us?

He said he would, but the week before we were to play in the All-Ireland final he got shipped off to the Congo with the army. It was all a bit of a mess.

We had to finance our own travel, for starters, and also cover any other expenses that popped their heads up. We managed to get a crowd to sponsor us, took a bus to the game, and we ended up winning well.

We wanted to get into the Harty Cup then but they wouldn't let us join. We played a few Harty Cup teams in challenge games and beat them, but we still couldn't get into the competition.

That still bugs me to this day.

The following year Patrickswell played Cappamore in the first round of the championship, which was my debut as a senior hurler.

A day I'll never forget.

I WAS JUST 16 years old. Cappamore were one of the top teams around, whereas we were still relying on a lot of young players. The half-back marking me was wearing a flat-cap, and wasn't shy of a few words.

He must have been delighted to see a young fella like me coming up against him. There was a bottle going around the pitch whenever there was a break in play, and judging by the way people were taking swigs out of it I had my doubts about whether the stuff inside was going to be in any way helpful in terms of hydration.

The bottle eventually made its way to yer man anyway, and after taking a big gulp he handed it to me.

'Take a swig out of that now… young man,' he ordered.

I obeyed.

It burned as it went down my throat. I politely declined a second swig.

Welcome to senior hurling.

Some of the lads felt we were out of our depth at senior level, and they wanted us to drop back down to junior so we could be more competitive. This was before the intermediate level was introduced, so we had to apply to drop down and play junior, and there were no guarantees that the application would be accepted.

The level we should be playing at became a point of consternation among the squad. Some felt that there was no point playing senior hurling if we weren't good enough to get to finals and win trophies. Others, including myself, felt that playing at senior level was the only way in which we would improve.

In the end, it went to a vote.

That ended in a tie.

Our chairman, Kevin Lynch, a very forward thinking man, had the casting vote and he decided that we would remain at senior level.

So that was that decided, but nobody really knew what the season ahead would bring. We managed to beat Claughaun, who were one of the top teams, in the first round. I would grow to become very familiar with my marker that day.

His name was Éamonn Cregan.

Claughaun would give us some of the fiercest battles down the years. One time we were playing against them in the Gaelic Grounds, and the match was abandoned when a row started. Peter, who is small enough as it is, was very young at the time.

That didn't stop him throwing himself right into the thick of the melee.

He looked like a little rottweiler nipping around the place and barking at people inside in the middle of the row. Mick Tynan was playing for Claughaun, and Mick didn't stand for much messing.

He caught Peter by the shirt and actually lifted him out over the fence, and told him to stay out of it so he didn't get killed. There was always rows in games, but very rarely would there be a red card.

The referee might take your name, but sure he could take it a few times during the one game and not do much else.

Anyway, that year we ended up getting to the semi-finals against a selection team from the south of Limerick.

In 1964, then, we were beaten in the first round by a last minute goal. Things didn't look particularly good for the club at that stage. We were good hurlers, and we had a decent set-up, but we needed to be doing more if we were to compete consistently.

By this stage my involvement had stretched beyond the pitch. I was assistant secretary, with Ger Casey as secretary. Ger always had brilliant ideas, and was always thinking ahead. He once put in a motion to the county board stating that every club should have to plant a certain amount of ash trees in order to keep the supply of hurleys at a healthy level. It shouldn't have been very difficult to organise, as most hurling clubs were rural clubs anyway.

Unfortunately, it never passed.

It would have involved way too much planning for the county board at the time.

I ENJOYED THE administrative side of things, but it was fairly easy going. It wasn't unusual to keep track of a meeting's minutes on the back of a cigarette box.

We had started putting more and more time and effort into our underage structures, and that had a knock-on effect across the whole club.

Treating every team, whether it was under-16s or senior, with a certain level of consideration made everyone feel like they were in it together, and it helped to bring the different factions of the club closer.

In 1965 we made a big effort across the board. We headed up to play a tournament in Croom before the championship. For one of the games we were short a full-back, and although I was only a whip of a lad at about nine stone, I got the vote to fill the slot. I was 19 and mad for hurling.

I would have played anywhere as long as I got to play. I stayed at full-back for a few games and although I did alright, we didn't fare too well as a team. Towards the end of the tournament I was pushed up to corner-forward, and managed to grab a couple of scores. We were sent packing shortly afterwards but the tournament was by no means a complete loss. For our troubles, we won ourselves a rather fetching set of Aran sweaters.

We were like the Clancy Brothers walking around the place for the next few months. Everyone could spot a Patrickswell hurler a mile off.

« CHAPTER 9 »

THE 1965 CHAMPIONSHIP was on the horizon, but it hadn't been decided if I would be best served staying at corner-forward or going back into full-back.

In the end they put me at full-back, and we went on to win our first senior championship. It wasn't much of a tactical masterstroke mind, as playing full-back was totally different to what it is today.

In the county final against St Kieran's, for example, everybody thought I had a great game, but I don't think I hit a single ball. You don't need to be Dónal O'Grady on *The Sunday Game* to analyse that.

My job was simply to keep out their full-forward, Pat Begley by whatever means necessary. With plenty of license to use my imagination. I managed to keep him under wraps on the day, but on another occasion he could have torn me to pieces.

That night we were bringing the first senior cup back to Patrickswell.

It was reasonable to expect the whole village would be out to greet us, but that wasn't the case. As it happened, there was a fundraiser scheduled the same night, and it was being held out in a big hall in Cappamore which had to be booked months in advance. We came back into Patrickswell with the cup, and there wasn't a sinner in the town.

Everyone was away off at this céilí to raise money for the club, so we had the run of the place to ourselves.

We hit the three pubs in the village, just the group of us, and then did the same thing the following night, when all of our family and friends were back to celebrate with us.

THE ALL-IRELAND club championships were still a few years away from being introduced, so we just entered the Munster championship. The first team we were due to play was Thurles Sarsfields. Most casual observers felt that the game would be a formality. We were in uncharted territory as a club, whereas Sarsfields had seven of the Tipperary team that had won the 1965 All-Ireland.

It was proper men vs boys stuff.

Jimmy Doyle, Paddy Doyle, Tony Wall, Sean McLoughlin.

These were household names. We couldn't even work out if our players were full-backs or corner-forwards.

The game was played in 1966 on a lovely crisp May evening in the Gaelic Grounds. Just before the ball was thrown in, our top forward, Eamonn Carey cried off injured. As a result, I was on the move again, and took up his usual centre-forward position. Somehow, we won the match with plenty to spare.

I finished as top scorer with 2-4, all of which came from play. I remember thinking that maybe centre-forward was the best place for me?

I loved it that day.

There was a bit of space to run into if I wanted to take off. I could hit a few scores, or I could join in the midfield battle. It felt like there was always something for me to do.

For one of the goals, I beat my man out to a ball around the 21 yard line, then took it all the way before burying it to the net. I never played full-back again.

It was one of those days where everything just clicked for us. There was this wonderful sense of rhythm within the team, as if we were all on the same wavelength. Sean Casey was in midfield for us and he didn't give Jimmy Doyle a puck of the ball. Sarsfields didn't know what hit them.

In truth, neither did we. We went back to Punch's Pub afterwards, which was also serving as our clubhouse. Paddy Barry was amongst the crowd there. I was a bit in awe of him, as he had trained All-Ireland winning Cork teams. He came over to me to shake my hand and say well done.

I felt on top of the world that a man of his calibre would take the time for a young fella like me. It was a special day.

The next challenge was a trip down to Dungarvan to play Mount Sion in the Munster final. Waterford had been in the 1963 All-Ireland final, and Mount Sion had supplied 11 of that panel. Frankie Welsh, Martin Óg Morrissey, Austin Flynn, Séamus Power... it was a serious team.

Even though we had beaten Sarsfields it felt like we were back to square one. It didn't feel like much of a reward for the upset we had caused in the semi-final. Even amongst ourselves, we didn't think we had much of a chance.

I was wing-forward, with Eamonn Carey centre-forward.

They hit us like a tornado. By half-time we were 10 points down. It might have been more actually, but I had long stopped keeping count. When we were losing badly, our half-time talks generally followed a similar rhythm. We never had an army of substitutes to fall back on, so the message was always to go back out there and give it one hell of a go, and see what happens.

Carey came off injured so my brother, Pat was put on. His introduction meant that there were now six Bennis brothers out on the pitch. The six of us standing on a field in Dungarvan, losing a Munster final by more points than I could remember.

This was not a highpoint for the family.

Now Pat wouldn't mind me saying that he wasn't the best hurler, but he could certainly stop a good hurler from hurling. Sure enough, he managed to keep Martin Óg Morrissey quiet, and with a strong breeze behind us we started to click and chip away at their lead.

We'd hit a point, win the ball back from the puck-out, and go get another point. Out of nowhere, we had hit our groove, and we could all feel it.

I was wishing that I had kept track of the score, because I knew we must have been closing in on them. We hit another point and one of our lads let out a massive roar. I was reliably informed that it was now a one-point game.

They got one back to give themselves a bit of a cushion as the clock wound down. We still had all the momentum, but time was against us.

Our goalie then gave away a soft free by going past his own '21' to take a puck-out. It was popped over the bar and Mount Sion won by three points, 4-10 to 4-7. I wasn't as effective as I had been at centre-forward against Sarsfields, as I saw a lot less of the ball. And I finished with 0-3.

WHILE THE HURLING was taking off in the club, the whole time we would still be playing a bit of football. In 1964 our junior footballers had won the city championship, which was a good achievement given we didn't really put much focus into football.

The semi-final was delayed until the following year, when we played Glen, who were a strong football club. The arrangement for football games was that you played one half with your opponent's football and the other half with your own.

The fact that we didn't actually own a football gives a fair indication of where football ranked in Patrickswell.

We ended up using Glen's ball for the whole game, and we beat them. They were disgusted to lose to a bunch of hurlers who didn't even own a ball, and found grounds to object. We had played Eamonn Carey and Jimmy Shields, who had both transferred down from Dublin to play senior with us.

To be fair, Glen were dead right to object, as the lads transferred in early 1965, but the game was still part of the '64 championship. That didn't stop us putting up a fight. We counter-objected, knowing full well that technically we were in the wrong.

Carey was a garda up in Dublin, and had been playing with Young Irelands. The way the objection process worked was we had to bring in the chap accused of being ineligible, and he had to be identified by the club who had filed the objection.

We found a fella from another club who looked a bit like Carey.

In we sent him.

The Glen lads lit up with anger and injustice as soon as he walked in.

'Yessssss… that's the fella!'

It was only when our stunt double had to confirm his name that they copped it wasn't Carey, but it was too late. The 'Well went marching on.

Our opponents in the county final were Croom.

They were another real football club. We realised that this was all getting a bit serious, so we decided to buy a football for that one.

We even did a few nights training in the build-up to the game, which was another new step for us. We were all mad excited to get going with our lovely new football. I couldn't wait to get down to training. I really enjoyed playing football, but it just didn't mean as much to me as playing hurling.

To me, football was almost a form of relaxation. I could just go out and enjoy it, without feeling any pressure. With hurling, winning and my own performance were far more important to me. We were so fit from hurling anyway that that often gave us enough of a base to get past some decent football teams.

Not expecting to be in a county football final, Phil had gotten married the Saturday before the game and was heading off to do the Ring of Kerry for his honeymoon. They only made it as far as Killarney on the first night, much to the confusion of Mary, his new bride. A night in Killarney had not been part of the itinerary. The next day, as they set off from their hotel, Phil turned the car around and broke the news that he was heading back to play the match.

I'm sure he's had more enjoyable spins in the car with Mary since.

There was a fella playing with Croom who worked with Phil, and knew of this plan to make it back for the match. He gave Phil an awful slagging before the throw-in, telling him that he looked awful shook for a man about to play a county final.

'We'll see who's shook when the match is over,' Phil fired back.

We won the game, but I'm not sure that justified Phil's decision in Mary's eyes.

« CHAPTER 10 »

PHIL LOVED THE club, and he was manager for 10, maybe 12 of the county titles that the senior hurlers have won. That's a record that Alex Ferguson would be proud of. He would have been instrumental for even more seasons, but he got involved with the county team in the late 1980s, and couldn't give the club his full attention anymore.

We had another two long serving managers in PJ Grady and Timmy O'Neill later on down the line. They were completely different characters.

Phil was a great motivator, but it's changed so much that I'm not sure his style would work now. Timmy was very good, very articulate and he brought a different approach to things. He was more interested in discussing different aspects of the game and the tactical side of things. That was a first for us.

It was simple enough stuff, we always thought.

He wouldn't want a corner-forward taking a shot from way out in the corner. He'd tell him to find a support runner, or play it inside instead. I loved talking with him about the different ways we could approach things.

AFTER WINNING OUR first senior county hurling title in 1965, we won it again the following year. There were six of us on the 1966 team.

Gerald was corner-back.

Phil centre-back.

Thomas left half-back.

Pat centrefield.

Myself centre-forward.

And Peter left corner-forward.

That was a big thing for all of us. We were a small knit community, and there was a sense around that we were overachieving given our resources. The two titles that we won in 1965 and '66 were claimed by a total of just seven households.

I'd say that the bond between us as brothers was never stronger than it was at that time. We've always been great friends, but we were really close back then. I suppose it would have been a disaster for the club if we weren't getting along. We were a very committed family.

I can say without any fear of contradiction that none of the six of us ever missed a training session for anything other than illness, and even that was very rare. We were always there. Even if we had just gotten married, in Phil's case.

I played the night before my own wedding.

There was nearly war. In the end I got the green light to play, but only if I stayed in goals. The logic was that that gave me the least chance of turning up for the big day with a limp or a black eye.

It was better than nothing, I guessed.

We lost the 1966 Munster club semi-final by a point to a strong Carrick Davins that had fellas like Mick Roche, PJ Ryan and TJ Ryan. We achieved nothing then in 1967, and around that time myself and a friend of mine, Willie Foley took over the juvenile club as chairman and secretary. To be honest I can't remember which of us was which.

Both of us were delegates to the city board and the county board. The club was our only interest really, apart from going to the odd dance. It controlled our lives, but we enjoyed it. We went to all the conventions, city board meetings and county board meetings.

The following year we made our breakthrough at underage level. We won the minor and under-21 county championships. I was training the minors and managing the under-21s. We always had really dedicated young lads, and they were good hurlers too. They were easy to train.

It certainly didn't feel like hard work to look after them, and there was nothing too technical about it. The sessions were the standard few laps of the field, followed by a bit of backs versus forwards until the lads tired. Any old Joe Soap could have done it, I just happened to be that Joe Soap.

But it did give me a taste for the management side of things.

THE 1969 LIMERICK senior championship brought more drama. This time, we beat Garryspillane but lost the game on an objection. Three of our lads, who had family connections in Kerry, had gone down to play a bit of club hurling there. They ended up winning an under-21 championship.

Garryspillane got wind of this, and filed an objection.

Our win against them had been one of our best performances. We were 11 points down at half-time but managed to turn it around in the second-half and beat them. We were all down in the pub celebrating when the club secretary came in and delivered the bad news. The window for objections was seven days, so they were just part and parcel of the game.

You'd nearly always find some auld reason to file an objection.

If you made any mistake, the other team would be ready to pounce and call you up on it. There were all these little rules you had to adhere too. One of them was that you had to have your team written out in Irish, and if it wasn't done correctly then the other team could object.

It was crazy. We came up against Garryspillane again the next year. Safe to say motivation wasn't an issue. We hammered them.

In 1969 we beat Pallasgreen by 0-17 to 2-3. I was centre-forward, and their centre-back wasn't the most mobile of fellas. In training we had devised a plan for me to get miles away from him, knowing that he'd struggle to stay in touch.

Unfortunately, some of our lads could sometimes be guilty of straying from or just flat out forgetting the plans set up during the week.

From our first puck out, he caught the sliothar and drove it down the field. The crowd started roaring at me to get tighter to him. I started making my way over to do just that, but our chairman bellowed over, 'If you keep heading over to him… you'll shortly be out here beside us'.

It worked out in the end.

I scored about 10 points.

In 1970 we beat Kilmallock in a desperately one-sided game. We were really going well as a team around that period. It helped that we had a few county players, because the step up between the club and county games was huge. With club hurling, you were always going to meet a few fellas who weren't really up to a very high standard, whereas with county hurling every opponent would at the very least be able to put it up to you.

You would rarely get to cash in on someone else's error at county level, but that would happen almost every game with the club.

The gap isn't as big now. Fitness was another issue for a lot of club players. There were plenty of club full-backs who wouldn't dream of coming out beyond the square. It was dream stuff for a forward with a bit of life in his legs.

You'd get to know opponents really well, because there would often be the same lads marking you every year. Of course, I had a brother playing for Ballybrown too, and we ended up on each other a few times. It wasn't the most comfortable of experiences, but there would be no blackguarding between us. We always beat them handy enough anyway so there was no real pressure on us in those games.

ONE OF MY favourite, and toughest, opponents was Éamonn Cregan, if that makes sense. We'd have ferocious battles, but he was just a magnificent hurler.

The first time I played with him was in 1963.

We were both minors, and we both ended up playing centrefield. I loved playing with him, but he was as tough an opponent as you could come across. There was a stage where he was centre-back for Claughaun, and I was centre-forward for Patrickswell.

We came up against each other quite often during that period. It was the same with Tom Ryan, who was centre-back for Ballybrown. Tom is a rare character. He was flamboyant, and could be careless with the hurley. The pair of us were sent-off in a city final once. It was my fault really.

We were beating them well, and I tried to take the mickey out of him. You'd get a good kick out of winding up Tom. I ran at him soloing the ball and tried to whip around him, so he threw a flake of a hurl and rapped me on the hand.

It was in the run-up to the 1974 All-Ireland final, and I didn't want to pick up a needless injury, so in the heat of the moment I turned back at him and there was a bit of a confrontation. The referee sent the pair of us off. There were headlines in the papers the following day saying that we would both miss the All-Ireland as a result. As it happened, we both received a one-month suspension, which had us back just in time for the final.

I didn't play well on the day. Tom didn't have his best game either. He was taken off, but I should have been benched before him. The county chairman came up to us afterwards and said that he should have given us longer suspensions. I'd say plenty in the crowd agreed with him.

The only other time I ever got sent off was in an under-21 semi-final in 1964. I deserved it too. There was a bit of hassle, the ref blew for a throw-in, and neither of the two of us went for the ball.

The ref just sent the two of us off immediately.

WE HAD GREAT success with the club during that period.

Between 1972 and '82 we ended up winning 10 city championships in-a-row. We would always have some tough games, but at times we felt untouchable. It was a shame we didn't do more beyond the city championship.

During that 10-year run we won three county titles, in 1977, 1979 and 1982. Even our best teams found it a real step up to go into the Munster club championship, however. We were coming up against teams like Blackrock, Glen Rovers, Clarecastle, Mount Sion, and they were all at their peak.

Tom Slattery of Clarecastle in Clare was one of the toughest opponents I came up against in club games. Jerry O'Sullivan was brilliant for Glen Rovers too, but Slattery was tough and dour. Munster was played during the winter so it suited a player like him more than someone like me. Defenders were nearly all tough or rugged.

The ball or the man would get by them. Never both.

The club hurling scene was very strong at the time, and you would be guaranteed good healthy crowds for any county finals. There was a fierce rivalry between club players too, because the club rivalries were so strong. You had about eight teams that could win the county on any given year, whereas now you only have three or four, realistically. We still mixed well when we went back into the county team.

For some reason the rivalries never carried into the Limerick camp.

In total I spent 24 years playing with the club, from 1962 to '86.

I went back for a short period after and played a bit of junior, winning a junior city championship against Na Piarsaigh, who were only a new club then.

My last game was against Pallasgreen in a junior county semi-final in Kilmallock, and we were beaten by a point. They went on to win it. I knew it was time to give it up then. It was bittersweet to stop playing but I had had a good innings, and was able to appreciate that. I'm almost certain that I only missed one championship match with Patrickswell through injury in all those years. I was very lucky. All the family were lucky actually.

I wouldn't say that my legs were going at that stage. I'd say they had gone a few years beforehand. I was grateful for the experience and memories the club gave me. The highlights were obvious, days that you'll never forget, but it's only when you sit down afterwards when you can look back and take some enjoyment from days that you wanted to crawl into a ball and go into hiding.

One of those days came when I had to fill in in goals for a game later in my career, when our main goalkeeper was injured. I thought I'd fly it, but I was hopeless. I had a good man in front of me in Leonard Enright, maybe the best full-back of all time, but even that was no good to me. Maybe I'd have fared better if he wasn't there, as a busy goalkeeper can usually pass the blame on to his defenders.

That's why Kilkenny rarely have All Star goalkeepers, they never have anything to do!

It's just a completely different science.

I was well able to strike a ball, but I couldn't even get my puck-outs right. The puck-out is an art in itself. Ciarán Carey was only young at the time so we stuck him in goals instead, deciding to make the young fella suffer instead of embarrassing the more experienced county man. We still beat Ballybrown!

ONE THING THAT never sat well with me was the fact we never had a clubhouse. Plenty of clubs wouldn't have had clubhouses, but with our success I felt we were in a place where we should be able to build one.

We finally got one built in 1980, and it was a fine facility. It's currently due to be refurbished, but it was a revelation at the time. We've also recently put in a new pitch to help accommodate numbers. We used to have a bar too, but there was no need with the three pubs in the village.

Lads were only coming up to the club when the pub closed so we had to introduce a rule to say there was no entry after a certain time. Then that turned into a rule that allowed only bar members and, eventually, we just abandoned it. It was too messy and too time consuming for what it was bringing in.

It could have all turned out quite differently. In 1963 there was an offer put on the table from Lord Harrington, our Protestant landowner with about 500 acres just outside the village. He gave good employment to the village at the time and was generally well liked.

There was a field that the club recently bought, which we had been trying to buy for an eternity. Lord Harrington offered to buy the field and the premises, which included a dance hall and a dwelling house; all adjacent to our pitch.

He offered £3,000, which was a fine sum of money.

If he bought it, we would have had a ready-made clubhouse, and a new field. Naturally some had their reservations about the arrangement. It went to a vote in the club and the casting vote went to the chairman.

'Long enough we were owned by the British,' he said.

He voted against it, and that moment changed the whole future of the club. For better or for worse, it is still up for debate.

The new facilities would have been a boost, but there were complications with our pitch too. Our pitch was used by the city board for fixtures because there was no other pitch in the locality, so if we had had a better pitch there would have been a lot more fixtures played out in Patrickswell. I'm not sure we would have won as many championships as we did if our pitch had ended up being a runway for half the county.

Gerald was chairman of the club for years and he ran a tight ship. He had two terms, the first of which was in the 1970s. Then in the 1980s we ran into about £80,000 of debt, which was the result of building the clubhouse and a few other costs. Sliothars and hurleys were costing us a fortune.

It isn't as bad now, thank God.

Gerald lived in town, right by Na Piarsaigh, so he would socialise around there. All of us would go there on St Stephen's night actually, because we had no clubhouse here. They were mad for Gerald to become chairman. He was great at delegating work. He would ensure that every member of the committee had a job to do.

Anyway, Kevin Lynch and Jimmy Carroll, two founding members, went up to see Gerald and pleaded with him to come back out and look after the club. He agreed, and in the four or five years he was there he cleared the debt, we won three senior championships in-a-row, two Munster clubs, and reached an All-Ireland club final. He got the whole parish working, and there was a great community spirit at the time, which washed over the team.

His work ethic trickled down through the team.

I STILL GO to any club match that I can.

I'm involved with the under-16s too. There are worse ways to pass the time. I had coached a few teams outside the parish previously too. I trained Kildimo-Pallaskenry, where Kyle Hayes is from.

I trained him a few years ago and he was bursting with potential, a lovely lad to work with. I get great enjoyment out of trying to help young lads improve their game. It's very rewarding. You can usually see the potential from a young age.

We've two or three very good players coming up through the ranks in Patrickswell at the moment. We're not that strong at underage currently, but that's not unusual for the club. I didn't win an underage game for Patrickswell until we beat Ballybrown, when I was 21.

At that stage I would never have dreamed of the success we would enjoy further down the line. I like to remind the lads of that every now and then if they're on a losing streak.

There's always hope.

PART FOUR

Life's Battles

PREVIOUS PAGE: Richie and Mary marry in May of 1971 (right), and Richie and Mary (with Imelda, Anthony and Alison) after Kieran and Laura wed in 2009. Middle: Richie and Mary with their children and grandkids.

IMELDA BENNIS
(Daughter)

DAD HAS ALWAYS been great fun, and he was always the lenient one. He was the one that when we got into trouble when we were younger, Mam would say, 'Wait until your Dad comes home', and then Dad would come home and say, 'You won't do that again?'.

We would say, 'No'.

And he'd go 'OK… that's fine so'.

He was the easy touch out of the two of them. Even now as a grandfather you might want him to correct the grandkids, but he'd say, 'No… you can't be giving out to them'. He's always been a soft touch with kids.

WHEN WE WERE growing up we wouldn't really have understood Dad being a Limerick hurler, and what that meant, but we had an idea that he was sort of 'famous'.

I remember breaking my hand when I was about seven years-old, and Dad brought me into the hospital to get an X-ray. We were walking down the hall and you could hear people whispering to each other, going, 'That's Richie Bennis'.

That's when I started to realise that he was more than just Dad.

I was never Imelda Bennis growing up.

I was always Richie's daughter.

You're never an individual. It's quite strange for a kid, but we knew that Dad was known for something positive so it was fine in that sense. There was probably an expectation that we would be good at the hurling or camogie, from others more so than from him, but unfortunately for Dad it didn't ring true in any of us.

He wouldn't have put any pressure on us to be great hurlers or camogie players either, but that was probably at least partially down to the fact that he was so involved with the game himself.

Even though none of us turned out to be very good at hurling, the house always revolved around hurling. Dad played well into his 40s, and then he was involved in training or selecting and all that, so there was always a match to go along to. We were dragged to a match every Sunday whether we liked it or not, and it only made life harder if you didn't want to go, but luckily we all ended up loving it and in that way it became part of all of our lives.

MAM WAS ALWAYS *the one that ran the house.*

She would have been the boss of the family because Dad was working and had the hurling and all that. The older they got, and as life threw Dad a few knocks, even though people say things like he's not afraid to mince his words, he's actually very soft.

He finds stress very hard, and Mam helps him deal with that. Mam has always been his rock though the hard times. She's amazing. But it's funny, you could say something to Dad, and if he's not sure he'll look at Mam and go, 'Is that good?'

She would tell him that it is good and he'd go, 'Oh that's great so'.

He's always sort of looked to her for reassurance.

He might not always listen though. For example, Mam was always a bit more wary of the press, whereas Dad would be more trusting. She would be telling him that everybody wants a story, so to be careful about how he gives them that story, but he'd just say, 'Ah they're grand'.

He's always been a big family man. Whatever about his own kids, now he adores his grandkids. He's a big child himself, and he spoils them rotten. He doesn't say no to them, and they're mad about him too. He's always been someone you could pick up the phone to, and he would do absolutely anything for you.

Then later on when he ended up becoming Limerick manager, we were just delighted for him because it was something that he always wanted. We were all so excited for him, and we ended up living through all the highs and lows with him.

It was very much a family affair.

HE WAS ALWAYS *active, but then he got sick and that set him back a good bit, but he became a different man when he got involved with Limerick again. It was like he got his identity back a little bit.*

He had gone from someone who was out doing things all the time to being stuck at home. Dad doesn't even like sitting down. He's always been mad to do something, to be good at something.

I remember him going to night classes for computers, and he'd go up to the girl giving the class at the end and ask her what they would be covering next week? Then he'd come home and get us to show him, so that he would be ahead of the game the following week!

So in that sense, being involved again with Limerick was brilliant for him.

The few years before that, it would be a stretch to say he was a lost soul, but it definitely gave him a purpose again. It made him feel alive again, and showed him that he had something to offer.

It made him more like himself again.

« CHAPTER 11 »

I'VE BEEN TRYING to work this out, but as far as I can remember I never actually proposed to Mary. Now that sounds worse than it actually is, because I remember plenty about the day itself.

May 23, 1971.

We had just beaten Tipperary in the league final down in Cork by a point, 3-12 to 3-11, and we were in the mood to celebrate. It was quite the milestone as it was my first league medal, and turned out to be my last, actually.

We were out enjoying the win that night, and by this stage myself and Mary had been seeing each other for some time. We were happy out together. That night, we agreed that we should get married. The timing seemed appropriate enough to me. By my recollection it was more of a conversation than a proposal.

Mary may correct me when she sits down to read this.

Myself and Mary had hit it off right away. When I first met her I was missing 12 teeth, so the fact that she gave me the time of day was a good sign. Maybe she reckoned she had something to look forward to.

I had been playing with Patrickswell against Adare, and when I was on the ground one of the Adare lads took a swing at me and his hurl caught me right on the mouth. I was fortunate he didn't do more damage. It was a proper dirty pull. Anyone who was there could see it was deliberate, and he ended up getting a five-year ban.

But, of course, he was back playing after 12 months.

The usual shite when it comes to appeals.

MARY AND I were both keen to avoid a long engagement, so we got married that summer. It was a very big wedding. The tradition in our family was that you invited everyone, and none of us wanted to be the one who broke the mould. I definitely didn't want to be known as the Bennis who didn't invite everyone to his wedding.

That kind of thing could put you in the bad books for life with some people.

We had a big enough guest list between the family, never mind friends and neighbours. Sure, there was 13 of us and all their offspring, just to get the numbers up and running. We were married in Castleconnell and had the reception in the Shannon Arms Hotel, right in the middle of the city.

The way things worked in our day was that you got married at 10.0 am, had dinner at 1.0 pm and everyone had to be out of the hotel by 6.0 pm. Because the room needed to be cleared for whatever dance was on that night. At that stage the wedding party would break up and you would head off to a pub, but quite often the newly-married couple would go on their honeymoon either that night or the next morning.

We had a fairly glamorous trip planned.

Mick Tynan, a great friend of mine, had invited us out to New York to play in an exhibition match, and the idea was that myself and Mary would use the trip as our honeymoon. I'd play in the game, and then we'd take a few days for ourselves afterwards.

What could go wrong with that?

Nothing, apart from Cardinal Cushing, who was a patron of the GAA in New York, dying. All GAA matches were cancelled. As was our honeymoon.

So that was that.

The back-up honeymoon was a tour of Ireland.

Not quite New York, but by no means a bad fall-back option. We started off in Galway, and then made our way up along the north-west coast to

Donegal, taking in all that wonderful scenery, appreciating the beauty of the island we live on. After a couple of days there we travelled across to Northern Ireland.

For both of us, it was our first time there. Mary wanted to go shopping so we headed for Coleraine in Derry. It wouldn't be my ideal day out but I was happy to go and see a new place. We drove into Coleraine and I parked the car right up near The Diamond, which is a big square in the middle of the town.

I was delighted with myself for getting a spot so close. We parked up the car and off we went to spend some money.

We came back out a little while later and no lie, there were about 20 soldiers standing around the car. We were terrified immediately.

They brought our attention to a nearby sign.

DO NOT LEAVE CARS UNOCCUPIED.

We had missed it when we drove in, not that we knew such rules existed. It was all very new to us. The southern registration on the car probably didn't help. When I think back on it, leaving a southern registration car unoccupied right in the middle of Coleraine in 1971 doesn't sound like my smartest idea.

To be fair the soldiers were dead nice about it.

They quickly copped that we were both frightened and embarrassed. They saw the confetti in the back of the car too and passed a few smart remarks, before letting us go on our way.

We didn't stay in Northern Ireland much longer.

That experience was harmless enough, but it did leave us a bit on edge. It opened our eyes to how little we knew about the situation up there. A bomb went off not too far from where we had booked to stay for the night, so we quickly cancelled our reservation and moved on. I found the whole time we spent there very intimidating.

We had our car searched coming over the border, and we both felt very nervous when we drove through Portrush and saw the curbs all painted blue, white and red. We were worried we would end up in a part of town where we weren't welcome. It's easy to forget just how tense it was in the North at that time.

OVERALL, THE HONEYMOON was wonderful. We came back home and began our new life as husband and wife. The next step was to start a family. Our first child, a son, arrived in 1973.

We named him Dickie. He was the most wonderful thing that had ever happened to us. It really felt like the start of an exciting new chapter in our lives.

The first remark when Dickie was born was... 'another hurler'. No-one ever mentioned the possibility of growing up to be a builder or a doctor or a lawyer or anything else. Just that he'd follow that great Bennis tradition and be a hurler.

The first few weeks whizzed by as we got used to being parents. Changing nappies, when to feed him, all of that, learning as we go. Mary did the bulk of the heavy lifting as I was off working and training. Still it was all working out fine.

Mary and Dickie and myself made a nice, happy little family.

It didn't take long for that perfect picture to be thrown into total fear and confusion. We had a babysitter looking after Dickie one evening, and when we came home she told us it might be worth getting him checked out. She knew kids well, and noticed that he was crying quite a lot and kind of arching himself.

That might have been something we would have noticed if we had any other children, but with Dickie being our first we didn't really know what was normal and what might be cause for concern. We arranged to go and see a specialist named Dr Basheer over in Castletroy. It cost £20 pounds per visit, which was a sizeable amount of money.

We didn't mind obviously and managed it. Dr Basheer only accepted the payment once and wouldn't take any payment after that. He was an absolute gentleman. He was actually following the story of Limerick reaching the All-Ireland final that year, and when he copped that I was on the team he paid a particular interest in us. He'd always be asking questions about hurling.

Dickie was about two months old when we first took him to see Dr Basheer. They did various tests but it took a while to figure out the issue.

After a few long, sleepless nights we finally received a diagnosis.

Dickie had cerebral palsy.

It was a huge shock. It took a lot out of me. I didn't really know what to do with myself or how to react. I was terrified, and upset.

Mary was much stronger.

She's always been that way. She was obviously devastated too, but she has always been great at facing those kind of things, and doing so much better than I can. She's that kind of woman.

Dr Basheer told us straight out as soon as they had it confirmed. We were really confused by the whole thing. We knew that it was a movement disorder, but we didn't know the extent of it or what type of quality of life Dickie could expect. We both thought that he'd be able to get up and walk around, but that was just based on seeing other kids with disabilities out walking around the town.

In reality we knew nothing of the severity of the disease.

We spent the next while meeting consultants and doctors and discovering more and more about cerebral palsy, but it took about six months before we got a proper picture of what the future would hold for Dickie. Getting some sort of clarity on the life he could expect to live was just as hard to take.

Dickie never walked, and he never managed to speak.

Mary minded him at home for the first five or six years, and then it got to a stage where she just wasn't able to provide the level of care that he needed.

Minding him was a full-time job. We were left facing some difficult decisions. We had to let Dickie leave home to go into full-time care. Our first born was gone from the house and still only a child. The place had never felt so empty. Mary found it tough to let go.

It was a very stressful and testing time. There are stages in a marriage where one of you really needs to be there for the other. God knows that Mary was always there for me when I needed her, but that was one time where she needed me. As upset as I was, my heart broke for her.

I felt helpless.

We both did. All we could do was be there for each other.

« CHAPTER 12 »

DICKIE WAS MOVED into a care facility in Kilkenny.

We went up to see him every weekend. It took him a while to settle there, which was difficult for us to see. It makes you question if it really is the right thing for him to be away from home?

After two years we managed to get him into a care facility closer to home, St Senan's in Foynes. They were wonderful with Dickie, and it definitely became a home from home for him. It put us at ease too to see the level of care and attention they gave him. They were absolutely top class.

It was only about a half an hour drive from our house, and so for the first while we were bringing him home for the odd weekend. They eventually told us that moving him to and from was only upsetting him, and that he would be better served by staying with them full-time.

That was another difficult day, hearing Dickie would probably never get to come home again, but we understood it was for the best. We went up to him every weekend, and anytime we were passing near Foynes we would call in for a bit.

We treasured those moments.

And I have some lovely memories of our time there with him.

We would just sit with him and talk. He'd recognise us without fully understanding who we were. My voice especially got a big reaction out of him.

I loved that.

It's hard to describe how it would make you feel to see the big smile on his face. He wasn't able to move his hands or hold anything, but he'd start moving them that little bit when we came into the room. That was his little way of acknowledging us.

It was very seldom that we would miss a weekend. We'd make it a family event and all head up together. The experience definitely brought our family closer, no question. All of his brothers and sisters adored him. We all felt a bit guilty that he was there too, even though we knew it was the best thing for him. It's just your instinct as a parent. There's a real sense of helplessness about the situation.

Mary always wanted to bring him home, but we all knew it would have been unfair on him.

CEREBRAL PALSY CAN be a dreadful infliction.

Dickie was fully formed and looked like a fine, big strong lad, but he never sat up in his life. He always had to be propped up, and he needed constant care. He had to be fed very regularly. The care in Foynes was so good that he only ever really got sick once or twice in his life. One time he had to be moved to the Regional Hospital, but that was it.

No matter when we turned up to see Dickie, during visiting hours or unannounced, the place was spotless and he would be getting the greatest of care. I'm eternally grateful to those people.

We were originally told that he would live to be 25 or 26, but not much older than that. But Dickie was a fighter. He reached that age, and although we had been made aware of his life expectancy we never really felt that our days with him were numbered.

He made it past 25, and his condition was stable. The years went by, and before we knew it he reached 30. It got to a stage where you almost forget that he wasn't expected to still be going.

Then one evening the call came.

We were all contacted and told that his condition was deteriorating, and that this was likely it. We made our way out to see him. One of our sons,

Anthony was down in Cork and had to travel up. We were all worried he wouldn't make it to Foynes in time.

We got there and explained the situation to Dickie, and asked him to hold on until Anthony arrived. Not to go before his brother had the chance to say goodbye.

The wait was awful.

Anthony finally made it to Foynes. He got to say his goodbyes, but he was barely in the room three minutes and Dickie died. That Anthony made it there gave us some sort of relief in a dark situation. The doctors said they couldn't understand how Dickie managed to hang on for that hour or so.

Like I said, Dickie was fighter. He lived to be 36 years old.

WE BROUGHT DICKIE home and laid him out in our house, back where he belonged. We buried him in Patrickswell the following day.

It ended up being a big funeral. The GAA is the furthest thing on your mind on a day like that, yet you get to see how the GAA community comes together in tough times. So many people that I wouldn't have expected to be there made the journey.

Eddie Keher came up from Kilkenny, for example. The GAA community is wonderful like that. JP McManus came too. It meant a lot that those people would take the time out of their day. It was a tough few days, but they sort of flash by in a blur.

It was a lovely mass. The top lady from Foynes, Niamh Finnucane gave a beautiful speech about Dickie, as if he was her own! It was heartfelt, and it was really touching to see the love that was there for Dickie. I think that meant a lot to all of us.

We knew they saw him as a person, rather than just a patient.

It's obviously very tough as a parent to bury your son, but at the time we didn't realise that the real struggle begins afterwards, when it is time to move on with life.

We had been in a such a routine with Dickie for such a lengthy part of our lives that, when he passed, it left a huge hole in our lives. Dickie had been such a central part of our schedule every week.

We didn't really know what to do with ourselves, and it took us quite a while to settle back into some shape of normality. We had extra free time, and that almost just opened up windows where you grieve, for the first while at least. Thankfully our other children were a wonderful source of support.

They knew how tough it was for us, but we certainly didn't underestimate what they were going through either. I've always felt lucky to have them in my life.

OUR FIRST DAUGHTER, Imelda was born the day I was playing a county final in 1974. I got a lot of stick over that because I wasn't there at the hospital. Truth be told, I don't think I would have been there anyway, match or no match.

I wasn't that kind of person and it wasn't really the done thing at the time. During half-time I got the news that I had my first daughter.

Great stuff!

We'll celebrate that later.

What's the plan for the second-half?

We won the match, and I raced off to meet the latest addition to the Bennis family. It was a great day.

She arrived just two years after Dickie, so naturally there was a bit of fear there on our part. We were worried she might not be born fully healthy, but thankfully everything went smoothly. Imelda works in IT now and lives just up the road from us with her fiancé, Mark and their two kids, Rian and Aoife, so we see them all the time.

Then we had Anthony, another fine, healthy young man. He's also grown up to be a wonderful man, and lives in Cork with his lovely husband, Padraig. He works in the world of computers and IT. They got married recently and we had a magnificent few days of celebration.

Anthony was a great kid, but had zero interest in hurling, which probably wasn't easy for him given his second name. When he went to do his oral Irish exam for the Leaving Certificate in 1994, the chap interviewing him copped the Bennis name.

He knew the connection with Gary Kirby, who was the Limerick captain at the time. He asked Anthony a few questions about Gary and about the

Limerick hurling team, but sure Anthony didn't follow it and had no clue what to say.

He didn't even know Gary was captain. He came home and told us that your man got awful embarrassed after thinking he had this handy subject to discuss.

Kieran was next. There were no problems with him during birth and we thought we had another healthy young boy, but when he was about six or seven months old we began to notice he wasn't really sitting up. It reminded us of what we had seen with Dickie, so we brought him to get checked and we went through that whole stressful process again. Eventually we were told that Kieran also had cerebral palsy.

Luckily Kieran is fine, and had a totally different situation to that of Dickie. We used to take him up to the Central Remedial Clinic in Dublin, and they were very good with him. Kieran's legs didn't form properly, and were kind of crossed, so we brought him for an operation in Cappagh National Orthopaedic Hospital, where they basically tried to straighten out his legs. They did an amazing job.

He's walking with crutches now but he drives his own car and the whole lot. He's married to Laura and has a good job with the HSE. Kieran has had a fine life. He's mad into hurling and comes to all the matches. Kieran plays in goals for the Munster wheelchair hurling team who won the All-Ireland in 2019. Kieran also won Munster Player of the Year the same season. You'd never relate his condition to what Dickie had, which just goes to show how complex an illness it is.

Then we had Alison, the baby of the family. Alison and her fiancé, Liam are living up the road with their daughter, Amy. Alison is the wild one of the bunch. We always knew she'd head off in search of adventure one day, and that it would have to be far, far away. Sure enough, that's exactly what happened. Alison is full of life and mad for the road.

She came into us one evening and told us she was going to head off to Australia with her partner for a while. They ended up being out there for five years altogether. We went over to them twice. I found Australia to be a great country... I didn't even mind the flight, which a few people had told me would be torture.

They had to spend three months working with a farmer, so we went out to see them there. Talk about being out in the sticks. We drove out to the middle of nowhere, and then just kept on driving for another few hours.

How they survived there, I have no idea.

The nearest shop was an hour's drive away, and the nearest pub was an hour in the opposite direction. If you headed out to grab some milk and go for a pint, you would lose half the day. They eventually came back and settled in Ireland, and Alison got a job with the council here in Limerick.

WE'VE BEEN FORTUNATE in that we've all gotten along great over the years. That's something some families maybe take for granted.

Myself and Mary have had a wonderful marriage. Funnily enough she knew nothing about hurling when she met me. I'd say she had never even been to a hurling match. When we started to see each other, it didn't take long for her to get an interest in it.

She probably realised she had no choice, living with me! There were a few perks that helped the cause too. I had promised her that I'd bring her to San Francisco if Limerick won the All-Ireland when I was playing, because the winning team would usually get a trip to the United States.

As it happened we won the All-Ireland good and early into our marriage, but Dickie was only six months old at the time the trip was planned. Everything had been diagnosed at that stage and we weren't sure whether to go or not. We eventually worked out that I would go, but Mary would stay as she didn't want to leave him.

A few people in the village knew the situation with the trip, and a woman named Mrs Moore called up to the house one day. She was a lovely, kind person, and Mary instantly warmed to her. She said she'd be delighted to mind Dickie.

Mary couldn't get on our flight at that stage but she came out the next day. We had a blast. It was the first time we properly got to switch off after all the worry that came with Dickie's situation. Then when we got home we called up to Mrs Moore but she insisted we take another day to ease back into things. It was a great break for us after all the stress we had been through.

I was well into my career as a builder by that stage. When I look at the professions our children fell into, it's almost mad to think of the world I grew up in. There are so many options for people now. I felt like I only had a handful of different career paths that were realistic when I was young.

One of the first jobs I ever went for was a position as a technician with An Post. I thought I might enjoy it, so I went along and did an exam for the job. There were 347 positions available, with around 100 of them in Limerick for some reason, many of them for juniors, so I felt I must be in with a decent shout.

I found the exam grand and shortly afterwards I was offered one of the jobs in Limerick. This was all good news, but then a few days later I was called up on a technicality. There was a rule that you had to be under the age of 17 on March 1 to be eligible. I had turned 17 on February 28. They wouldn't bend the rule so the job offer was rescinded and I was back to the drawing board.

I then started doing some work for a company that sold clothes house to house. I'm not sure how I ever considered that to be a good idea.

I absolutely hated every minute of it. I wasn't much of a salesman, and if someone wasn't interested in buying the clothes I had to offer, then I wasn't of much of a mind to try persuade them otherwise. I'd spend the whole day making my way around Limerick, trying to make a sale, and often end up with nothing to show for it. I got no satisfaction from it at all.

I didn't last too long before packing that in, and the company weren't too disappointed to see me leave. I was no loss to the fashion industry, and all parties involved were very much aware of that.

THAT'S WHEN I went into building, and I instantly loved it.

There were always jobs to be done somewhere or someone needing a hand on a site, so it was handy enough to get into. I actually found it quite relaxing, and never really felt under any great pressure with the workload. I liked having a project to work on, with a clearly defined start and end point.

There was a nice structure to it. Building is almost like completing a big puzzle. You put all the parts together and then you end up with the finished product. You can do your work, then step back and see the results first hand. I find that very fulfilling.

It's maybe no wonder I enjoy doing jigsaws so much. Building a house and doing a jigsaw aren't too far removed. As soon as you come into our house, I have a big jigsaw that I completed a few years ago framed and hanging. It's a photograph of the whole family. I've always enjoyed the process of them. I can easily sit there and while away the hours putting a jigsaw together.

With building, I also loved the fact that at 5 o'clock, it was time to go home. Some people spend too long working, up and out the door early in the morning and then coming in late at night.

Life is for living, not working.

When I was selling clothes, I felt like I'd never get home. I was always left chasing targets, or feeling guilty about finishing up at the end of the day if I didn't have enough to show for it.

It also helped that there was plenty of work in building.

You'd never be short of a bit of work if you needed it. There was a chap who lived over the road named Paddy Foley, and I used to head off with him in the evenings and do a bit of extra work. You'd always find extra work on a Saturday or a Bank Holiday too if you needed it. It helped ease some of the expenses that came with Dickie's situation.

I carried on building when I retired from playing hurling, and I could give a bit more time to it then. I wasn't as fit as I used to be, but it was nice to be able to work on a site without the usual bumps and bruises the day after a game.

« CHAPTER 13 »

IN THE 00s, when the kids were all grown up, or getting there, life eventually fell into a nice rhythm as we began to deal with the pain of losing Dickie.

I'd work during the week, get home at a reasonable hour, have dinner with the family and then sit around watching TV or doing whatever. At the weekends then, we might head off for a drive, and there would always be matches on.

Things began to feel somewhat normal again.

Yet none of us ever know what's around the corner. The family would soon find themselves back in the rhythm of hospital calls and sleepless nights.

ANYONE WHO HAS worked on a site would be able to tell you that a few scrapes and bangs are simply part of the job. You wouldn't exactly be whacking a hammer off your thumb like you might see in cartoons, but you'd often bump a knee off something, or drop something on a foot. It's just part and parcel of manual labour.

One day, in 2003, I was out on a job, and was up on some scaffolding. I took a step back from what I was working on, and caught my side off a knuckle that sort of jutted out from the scaffolding a small bit. It was a very innocuous bang, like catching yourself off the edge of the kitchen table.

It stung a little, so I gave it a rub, cursed myself, and carried on tipping away. I thought nothing of it. I'd often hit myself a lot harder on a job. I'd definitely had worse bangs on a hurling pitch.

I carried on anyway and then a little while later I started to feel a bit dizzy. Nothing major, but just a little bit off. I sat down and took a few minutes to gather myself, then shook it off and got back to work.

After a little while I found myself starting to feel a bit confused.

I realised that I was a little unsure of where I was or what I was supposed to be doing. I thought maybe I was coming down with a bug, and I didn't fancy the idea of getting sick on the site. I told one of the lads that I wasn't feeling right and that I was going to head off home early and rest up.

I hopped in the van and drove home.

It was a decent spin as I was out working on the other side of Limerick. To this day I don't remember leaving the site or anything of the drive home. When I got in the front door and Mary saw me, she rang the doctor immediately.

We went up to see the doctor and after a quick examination she told me it wasn't anything to worry about. She gave me some tablets and I was off back home again. I don't think it helped that the incident happened on a Friday.

In this country you're not supposed to get sick on a Friday.

I still wasn't feeling well so I just hopped into bed and hoped that I might sleep it off. I was out like a light the minute my head hit the pillow. When I woke up the following morning I lay there and took a few minutes to gather myself, and thought that I felt alright. I made moves to get out of bed, but when I turned to get up it was like I flicked a switch inside me.

Suddenly I couldn't function at all.

I got really dizzy, very quickly. I tried to gather myself, but I couldn't even focus enough to get my trousers on. At that point, I knew something wasn't right.

Peter got me into the car and we headed straight to the Regional Hospital. By the time we got there I was barely functioning. It was a busy Saturday morning in the hospital, and I couldn't really make sense of the fuss that was going on around me as the lads tried to get someone to see me. Luckily a good friend of mine was working quite high up the ladder in the HSE, and he helped get one of the top consultants down to look after me.

That helped to move things on that bit quicker. They were able to diagnose me with septicemia, which is basically when a bacterial infection enters the bloodstream. The bang on the building site seemed to have somehow ignited it.

I spent the next six weeks in ICU.

It was very touch and go. At one stage they were considering taking my leg off because the poison was travelling so fast throughout my body, and they were struggling to get it under control. About two weeks into my stay in ICU, the family were off at a wedding and got a call to say that I was losing the battle.

THEY ALL RUSHED out to see me, thinking that it would be for the last time. The doctors told my family to hope and pray, but they never gave up on me and eventually my condition gradually improved. Eventually I got over the worst of it. The doctors could barely believe I had come through the other side. They later told me that it was a million to one chance that I survived.

Most of the panic was lost on me at the time, as I don't really remember anything of those six weeks. There are only two moments that I have any recollection of. I can vaguely remember one of the doctors at the end of my bed saying, 'We won't take his leg off just yet'.

I have a much clearer memory of hearing another doctor say, 'Well, it's not cancer anyway'. I can remember feeling a rush of relief when I heard that.

Yet those are the only two moments from the six weeks I can remember. I can remember feeling unwell on the site, going to the hospital the next day and then just coming around a few weeks later with the worst of it behind me, and the family filling me in on what had happened.

It was like having a tiny chunk of your life erased.

In total I spent two months in hospital, before I was finally well enough to be allowed go home. Even though that should have been a great day, everything about my life felt different. I wasn't even that happy to get out of hospital because my head felt so scrambled.

Mary came and collected me. We gathered my few bits and walked out of the hospital and headed for the car. I stopped and felt the fresh air on my face, relieved that I was deemed healthy enough to leave.

Then I looked around me, and realised that I didn't recognise anything that I saw. I couldn't identify the area at all, even though I'd been there countless times over the years. There was a pub across the road, The Unicorn which I had been in a number of times, and I stared at it trying to figure out what it was.

I couldn't place it at all.

On the drive home I looked out the window as we passed by places I knew my whole life, trying to put the pieces together of where I was and where we were going. It was like I had been dumped in some strange new land for the first time.

Getting back home should have been the start of the recovery, but it just felt like the start of the next struggle.

For a long time I felt completely drained of energy.

Everything felt like an effort, physically and mentally. Personally, that was what I found the hardest, because I had always been a very active person. I was always mad to get up and do something, and now I couldn't even muster up the energy to just go outside. I felt trapped in the house.

This lasted for the guts of six months, and the longer it went on, the more I slipped into a state of depression. This wasn't the type of life I wanted, sitting around not doing anything, not feeling like I wanted to do anything. I can't imagine how Mary felt seeing me like that.

I was a totally different person, with no drive or motivation.

I didn't eat properly for months, which didn't help with the fatigue. Not only did I have no appetite, food just didn't seem appealing to me. There was nothing you could put in front of me that I would want to eat.

Mary kept going to the trouble of cooking me all these different lovely dinners, and I'd just sit there pushing my food around the plate like a grumpy child. The only thing keeping me going were yogurts. I found them easy to eat because they were so gentle on my stomach, and required very little effort to eat.

The doctors had told me that I would never be able to go back to work, and that was hard to hear. It was a full stop on a huge part of my life. I was thinking that even if I did get better, now I would have no job to go to. It took away what would have been a real motivation for my recovery, something to work towards.

Some days felt like they would never end.

Flicking through the newspaper, staring at whatever was on the television. I found myself just trying to get through each day, lying around in bed, feeling increasingly depressed. People were worried about me.

I was recommended a good psychiatrist by somebody I trust, but I had no interest in talking to a stranger about the way I felt. That sounded like a massive effort, given I could barely even leave the house.

BOTTLING THINGS UP was only serving to make me feel worse.

Eventually I started telling Mary how I really felt, and I found that that helped. Just talking about it lifted some of the weight off me.

Before that, I didn't think I needed to talk to anybody about what I was going through, but then I realised that I had access to the best psychiatrist money couldn't buy, and that she was living under the same roof as me.

I would sit down and talk out how I was feeling with Mary, and that helped me to feel better about my situation. I started to open up to her more and more. She knew the right things to say to me, to help me get motivated again, and I was comfortable telling her anything.

Some people might think I should have gone to a psychiatrist, but talking to Mary was easier for me. I also think it was important that I knew she had my best interests at heart. Sure there was nobody in the world who knew me better. I know for a fact I wouldn't have spoken as openly with a psychiatrist.

Very slowly, I started feeling increasingly determined to get myself out of this rut. The first time I tried to break the cycle was about six months after I had taken ill. I was using a walking stick at the time, and managed to get out and walk up to my sister-in-law, Patsy's.

It was only next door, but it took me a fair while.

I made sure not to rush myself. Getting there was the only thing that mattered. As I got up to her front door, I got a smell of something cooking coming from the kitchen. I immediately recognised it as bacon and cabbage.

That had always been my favourite meal, and when I called in she fixed me up a plate. I wolfed it down. From that day, I was back eating properly again. Mary had cooked bacon and cabbage for me a few times but I wouldn't even taste it. Maybe it was just coincidence that day at Patsy's, or maybe the walk had triggered my appetite back into action.

While that was a big milestone, the recovery was still a slow process. There was very little that I could do without feeling totally shattered. At one stage a fella came out from one of the local papers looking to do some sort of interview, for some reason, even though I was in no real mood for it. I don't know why I even agreed to it.

Maybe I just wanted to hear a different voice. We got talking about my health anyway, and he said to me, 'Jaysus Richie, do you know if you died now, I'd say you'd have the biggest funeral Patrickswell has ever seen'.

It was an odd thing to mention.

I needed to keep away from that type of thinking.

ONE DAY I was sitting around the house, wondering how to kill another few hours, and suddenly I felt this massive sense of frustration come over me.

I'd had enough.

I threw on a coat and headed off in the direction of Patrickswell.

The journey is about a mile and quarter from the house. It was way further than anything I had managed in the previous six months.

I felt tired, but determined that I was going to make it.

I told myself that if I wasn't out doing this now, I'd only be at home feeling sorry for myself. I was the only person who had the ability to change things, and I had nothing to lose.

The worse-case scenario was that I'd have to stop in somewhere and ring someone to collect me. I was determined that that wasn't going to happen.

My legs quickly began to ache, but I just kept going.

I'd pass one little landmark, mentally tick it off, and remind myself that I was getting closer and closer.

I thought of all the times I had walked those roads before.

I thought about how short a drive it was.

Repeatedly, I told myself that I could do it.

I reminded myself that I had been doing it all my life.

Eventually the town came into sight, but even that last stretch felt like an age. At this stage of my life, I guess that's the closest I'll ever come to feeling like a marathon runner coming down the home straight.

I couldn't believe it when I actually made it to the village.

The sense of achievement wasn't like anything I had felt before. Half of me felt stupid for being so happy with this walk, but the other half felt like I had conquered Everest. I guess I had conquered Everest in my own way.

It's all relative.

I was talking to anybody and everybody that I saw. Sure, no-one had seen me out of the house in months. I don't think I've ever been so popular!

I soon had to sit down somewhere and call Mary to come and collect me, but I had done it. That kick-started my recovery properly. Soon I was out cutting the lawn again. It felt great to go outside and do that for half an hour. Those little things felt like huge achievements. Each time I'd sit down afterwards and tell myself I was on the right path.

I was beginning to feel like myself again, but it was two years before I felt truly right. The first time I drove since getting sick we were up in Clonmel. It was me, Imelda and Mary, and we had a lovely walk up around the orchard there. I was enjoying the day and the fresh air, and as we headed back to the car, I told the girls that I felt well enough to drive home. I took the keys and sat into the driver's seat, but when I settled into the car I looked around and didn't know where to start.

I couldn't make sense of where I was and what I was trying to do.

I didn't know where to put the keys, or what I needed to do first, or even where to put my hands. I accepted defeat and swapped into the passenger seat. It had given me a real fright. I thought I might never be myself again.

NATURALLY THAT PERIOD totally changed my outlook on life. When I started feeling better, I had a new-found appreciation for everything that I had.

I suppose one of the biggest challenges was that there was no money coming in. This was 2003 remember, so the building industry was booming. There was huge money to be made. Some lads I knew were getting €2 a block and earning €300-400 for a Saturday.

We got over losing out on that because it was the least of our problems, but we did have to make readjustments.

It was only three years later that Limerick came calling and asked me to manage the county team, so life quickly turned on its head again. The doctors didn't want me to do it, but my feeling was that a challenge like that would only serve to energise me, which turned out to be the case.

Those few years ended up being the most alive I had felt in a long time. My illness wasn't a big deal at that time, publicly, which had its pros and cons.

In 2008 we played a league match against Galway in the Gaelic Grounds, and I had just gotten a pacemaker in on the Friday before the game. The doctor told me to skip the game, which I think he knew was never going to happen, so we reached a compromise that I would go and just not get involved.

I gave Gary Kirby my bainisteoir bib and I sat up in the stands for the game.

We ended up losing, and one reporter wrote that the pressure was getting to me. He wrote that I wasn't able for the sideline anymore and had lost my nerve, getting Gary to call the shots instead. I thought about calling him out on it, and was pissed off that he had made no attempt to clarify the situation with me, but then decided against it.

I decided that I was secure enough to ignore any nonsense in the papers.

It just didn't seem like something that was worth any of my energy. Once you've come through a genuine battle, those things don't even dent the armour anymore. There are bigger problems in life.

PART FIVE

Property of Limerick

PREVIOUS PAGE: The Limerick team that defeated
Kilkenny in the 1973 All-Ireland final

ÉAMONN CREGAN
(Limerick teammate)

RICHIE AND MYSELF played on a minor team together in 1963, but in those days you didn't really know too many of the other players on the team.

You knew a few lads that you might have gone to school with, but you wouldn't have known the rest of the players. The first time we really would have got to know each other would have been in 1966, which is when we played under-21 together. Not long after that, Richie very much came into prominence with Patrickswell because they started to win championships in Limerick, and Richie was one of the key players which formed the backbone of that Patrickswell team.

What was Richie like as a teammate?

Well, he didn't hold back. If he thought you were an eejit he would call you an eejit, and if you were a fool he would call you a fool. But it was all in good form.

The craic in the dressing-room in those days wouldn't have been great, because you had the county lads who would be sort of sticking together, and then the same with the city lads. Even though Patrickswell were in the city division, they were still regarded as 'county'.

But as we went on, from 1966 onwards, myself and Richie got to know each other very well, and we played on the same teams for years and years.

When we came in around 1966, we were both only 21.

People like Kevin Long and Éamonn 'Ned' Rea would have been the strong presences on the senior panel, so we tended to keep our mouths shut and just listen to those lads. As things progressed, and we got to our first league final in 1970, our group started to come into our own.

By that stage we were 24 or 25, so we were beginning to mature. Every one of us had our own ideas on how the team should be playing, and how good or how bad Limerick were. Richie had his views and I had my own, and we'd often throw them around. We intermingled in that sense.

WE WOULDN'T HAVE been similar personalities.

I would have been regarded as stand-offish. In those days I was quite shy, which people wouldn't believe now. But I was quite shy, and Richie was kind of an extrovert.

He'd throw out the odd comment to wake you up if he felt the need. There wasn't much shyness in Richie.

He would have preferred to have played a different type of game than I would. We would discuss that too. It would never develop into an argument, but we would discuss things like that.

I would have been of the belief that you should constantly be moving the ball on quickly. My ideal centre-forward play would be to keep the ball moving, and get it into the full-forward line, so as not to let the half-back line settle.

Richie would do that to a certain extent, but he would also want to occasionally lift balls and either try to move it on himself or try and get a score himself.

Richie first of all was a free-taker, and from that free-taking he got tremendous confidence in his ability to score and in how he could put balls over the bar.

So there was a difference in opinion there between the two of us. I wanted fast ball constantly, but he was willing to stop the ball and slow the game down. If he felt there was an opportunity where he could put the ball over the bar, he was happy to go with that.

We came from two different angles.

Those of us who would have gone to CBS Sexton Street played a different brand of hurling. We always played fast hurling that involved moving the ball very quickly. Richie came from a different background, where you played with the ball more before you moved it on.

You could see that difference between lads in the team at the time. At some stage we had to all come in on a certain style of the game, and everybody then rowed in behind that.

MYSELF AND RICHIE weren't just team-mates of course, and I had many a battle with Richie through our clubs as well. And let me say here and now, every battle that I ever had with Richie was fair and square.

There was no dirty play, there was no mouthing to each other or anything like that. Okay, he might give out if I got a free against him and I might do likewise, but there was never a dirty pull.

Whenever we stood up to each other and faced each other, I always found a fair opponent.

« CHAPTER 14 »

YOU MAY SPOT a trend in this book that very little has come to me in a straightforward fashion. That can be traced right the way back to my first appearance as a minor hurler, which came under rather unusual circumstances.

I had been selected on the Limerick minor panel in 1962, but I was quite young compared to most of the lads and found it difficult to get on the pitch. The following year I was left off the panel completely, reduced back to the role of spectator.

The Limerick minors were playing Galway up in the Gaelic Grounds, and I was thumbing a lift into the match with a pal of mine, Davy Moran.

The two of us were waiting along the side of the road, hoping some kind soul would pass our way. Just as our thumbs were starting to ache, a car pulled up.

Our lucky day.

Even better, there was a familiar face in the driver's seat.

Tommy Casey drove a taxi and would come out and collect people to bring them into the match. Turns out, Tommy was as happy to see us as we were to see him. He had been sent on a mission to find us.

We were told to hop into the car immediately, and Tommy put the foot down. It had emerged that three of Limerick's players were overage, so they were short for the game. Not only was I heading to the Gaelic Grounds, I was now togging out at left half-back.

We beat Galway, but the whole day was a bit of a blur.

All that I cared about was the fact I could now officially consider myself a Limerick player. I felt 10 feet tall. We were through to the All-Ireland semi-final, and not only was I kept on the team, but I was moved into midfield, lining out alongside a lad from Claughaun by the name of Éamonn Cregan.

It turned out he was a handy enough hurler, but it wasn't my greatest display in a green jersey, to put it mildly. We managed to steal a draw but I was dropped for the replay. It was no great surprise to me.

I'd gone from thumbing a lift, to starting in midfield to being dropped in the space of just three games. An early education in how quickly fortunes can change in the world of sport.

The lads beat Waterford and so we were in an All-Ireland final, playing Wexford in Croke Park. It was dream stuff.

LIKE ANY YOUNG fella I was dreaming of getting to run out on that famous turf, but it didn't take long for circumstances outside of my control to burst my bubble on the day of the game.

We lost both our goalkeeper and a corner-back to injury in the first five minutes of the game. Only three substitutions were allowed in the game, so that more or less immediately ruined any chance I had of getting a run out. Wexford beat us, and that was the end of my minor career.

I also played under-21 between 1964 and 1966, during which time the county didn't have a great innings. The real advantage for me was that I had joined the senior panel in that time, so the under-21 games were great in terms of helping to develop my game for senior inter-county hurling. There was less pressure but the quality was still high.

We played Cork in the 1966 under-21 Munster final, where I was centre-forward. They had 11 of the Cork team that had won the senior All-Ireland championship earlier that year. Despite that, they only barely beat us on the day.

My first taste of senior inter-county came against Clare in 1964.

I was 19.

The game was played in Tipperary, which would not be unusual for Munster championship hurling, except for the fact that it was set for Nenagh, rather that Thurles. That kind of tells you how much interest there was in that particular fixture.

You wouldn't even fit the backroom teams in if Limerick and Clare played a senior game there now. Imagine telling somebody like Davy Fitzgerald that he had to go to Nenagh for a Munster championship game?

As it happened, I didn't get a run out anyway and we were hammered, 4-14 to 2-6.

The following year I was handed my debut in the final round of fixtures during the group stage of the league. I was extremely nervous of course, my first official game for Limerick. Éamonn Cregan scored 2-4 that day, but we still lost 4-10 to 3-6.

It was a huge moment for me personally, but it was a slightly strange day. I didn't really know the other players in the squad that well because the group would only ever meet up for county games, and there weren't too many of them. There wasn't a huge amount of training done in the build-up to games either.

You often just met up a few nights before the game and did two very basic sessions.

Still, it was a great buzz to be a part of it all.

I was kept on the panel for the championship, and we played Waterford down in Cork. I relished being involved, and savoured every moment of the day.

The trouble was, we lost, so that was it for another year.

That always made those early defeats so disappointing. You get a taste for summer championship hurling and then it's gone for a whole year again. I'd have loved a qualifier system back then. Still, from that year on I was more or less a regular in the team.

In 1966 we were back together for a Munster quarter-final meeting with Tipperary down in Cork. That Tipperary team was like the great Brian Cody Kilkenny teams of the 2000s, and were hot favourites having won the All-Ireland the previous year. I was a substitute, but we pulled off a major shock and won.

It's funny how the game works. That Tipp team were superstars having won back-to-back All-Irelands, but they haven't won back to back titles since.

ÉAMONN CREGAN WAS being marked by Mick Burns, a great hurler, yet Éamonn still scored 3-5. We were starting to notice that there was something a bit special about Éamonn. He had been captain in 1963, but was really taking his game up a level now.

Not only could he score a bagful all by himself, but he could run a game and change the outlook all by himself. Next up was a Munster semi-final against Cork, in Killarney. I was really excited obviously, but disaster struck.

About three weeks before the game, I broke my thumb. The worst thing was it happened playing football. The only time I ever missed a senior Limerick game, and it was because of a football injury.

Cork beat us by two points.

My championship action was limited in the early days, but I was playing in nearly all of our league games. This was still when the league started in October and ran over into the following year.

Our first championship match of 1967 was in Thurles against Clare, and I had gotten a good few minutes under my belt throughout the previous league campaign. I started at corner-forward and we lost 3-14 to 2-7, but I took some small solace in the fact that I was our top scorer with 1-2. I was starting to feel like I was finding my feet in the team.

The following year represented another step up in terms of my responsibilities within the team. Éamonn had been Limerick's free-taker up to that point, but he missed a couple that year. We lost to Cork 3-11 to 2-9 in Thurles, and it was decided that I should be given a shot at taking the frees. There was no big discussion or anything. I was taking them for the club and doing alright, so I think it was just to try something new.

In 1969 we felt we were starting to move in the right direction. We reached the semi-finals of the league but lost to Wexford, but then we went out in the first round of Munster after a defeat to Tipperary.

Around that time then there was a bit of upheaval with the county board. They weren't happy with the results over the last few years, because we had plenty of talent. They had a point too. They brought in a guy from Down named Joe McGrath, who had come down to Limerick for work and joined the hurling club out in Claughaun.

Joe came to the county board and presented them with a five-year plan.

He told them that he would guarantee Limerick would win an All-Ireland within five years. It was looked on with scorn by some people who didn't like the idea of an outsider coming in and telling Limerick what to do. Others just saw it as wishful thinking. Anyway, Joe got the job.

That changed everything for us.

Actually, 1970 turned out to be a major year for me too. I was on the Munster team, and we were given a trip to America by Cardinal Cushing, who was the patron of the GAA in New York at that time. We went over, but we were just after buying a car so money wasn't very plentiful.

Anyway, I bought a ticket.

My sister was very involved in the foundation of Wolfe Tones in Shannon, where she lives. They were selling tickets for a sweepstake in the English Grand National, three pence each or four for a shilling.

The horse I drew, Gay Trip went on to win by 20 lengths, ridden by a Dublin jockey named Pat Taaffe.

I won 50 pound, and I decided that would be my trip money.

We had three weeks, and took in New York, Connecticut and Boston. I befriended a Limerick fella over there by the name of Corbett, who owned three pubs. We became very close friends. He had no family, and he told me that if I was to stay in New York, he'd give me one of the three bars.

I was very tempted, but the lure of hurling brought me home.

« CHAPTER 15 »

I LOVED NEW York. It was like being in a different world.

You had all the associations over from the various Munster counties, and they all gave us a free night, which was basically a wallet handed to us and we could do whatever we wanted with the cash. I'd say some of the lads didn't even see the streets, it was just the door of one pub to the next. I had a brilliant holiday and actually came home with more money that I went out with.

We were given special blazers and the whole lot, and we were staying right on the corner of Times Square. There was no food in the hotel, so we'd stick on our blazers and head to a place across the road for pancakes and the whole works.

The first morning we had a lovely waitress serving us, and we thought we were all getting along great. The following day, we went back in and she never came near us. We eventually worked out we had never tipped her.

We didn't even know it was a thing. That was one of many small cultural differences we learned over the three weeks.

It was one of the reasons I thought seriously about taking on one of Corbett's bars. One night, I was there with Willie Walsh and Gerald McCarthy, two of the Cork lads, and he took us in and showed me what they had made in tips alone.

I still love to visit New York, but I don't think I would have been cut out for the pace of life there. Anyway, what good are all those tips if you can't play county hurling?

WE HAD A great run in the league in 1969-70 and went all the way to the final. To get there we had to play a great Offaly team in the semi-finals in Thurles.

I had been dying with the flu going down to the game, and it was very doubtful whether I'd be able to play or not. I felt dog rough. Before the game, one of the county board officials came up to me and handed me some sort of potion, and told me to get it into me.

I necked it without questioning him.

I never found out what it actually was, but I was a new man after taking it. We won 4-15 to 2-8, and I scored 2-9.

It was one of those days where everything just went right for me. They don't come around too often, and over the course of my career I began to appreciate them more when they did come.

I was going with a girl inside in town at the time, and had arranged a date with her for that night. When I got home from the match, the flu hit me again like a bus. It was as if the match had been some little window where the sickness had left me. Now I was back feeling even worse than I had that morning.

I climbed into bed and sent Peter in to tell her that I wouldn't be coming into town to meet her. You can imagine how that news went down given she had heard about my performance against Offaly just a few hours beforehand. She was convinced I had headed off out celebrating with the lads, and she didn't speak to me for about 20 years.

We played Cork up in Croke Park in the final but they beat us well, 2-17 to 0-7. I was centre-forward, with my brother Phil at right half-back and my other brother Peter at right corner-forward. There was a Bennis in every direction I looked. We were disappointed to lose the final but that year we had started to see a difference under Joe.

He was certainly improving us as a group. I was also growing as a player the whole time, and I ended up as the top scorer in the league with 3-36.

Joe's five-year plan had brought a new dimension to our training sessions.

When he came in, we would have been lucky to have two or three sliothars at training.

Joe insisted that we would always have 12.

The county board was so shocked by this demand that I'd say there was nearly a special convention called. Their thinking was, 'Why on earth would a team need 12 sliothars?' But Joe saw things differently, especially for that time, and he wasn't afraid to be persistent. He got his way, and the new sliothars were there waiting for us one evening.

The next thing he turned his attention to was what we were putting into our bodies before matches. We were only training a few nights before a game, and we would all get a glass of milk and a sandwich after.

The sandwich wouldn't always be too fresh either.

I'm not sure how he swung it, but Joe knocked that on the head and got us into the Shannon Arms for steak dinners. We felt like kings. The county board were shocked by these new expenses, but they were getting the results on the pitch that they had been demanding. Once the results kept coming, Joe was going to get his way.

We would train harder with the club than we would with the county in the early year. That all changed when Joe came in. Joe was before his time. Even in those days, Joe would show us videos of matches and break things down for us.

He put more structure on our training. We would start training for the championship in February, and from day one we were running drills and playing in-house matches. Before that it had only been a puck-around. Joe would bring in extra players and we would have a full-on match.

We could all see that Joe didn't actually have much of a clue about hurling, particularly in the early days, but he was a great organiser. Sometimes that's all you need. Joe was a football man, but he knew that a little planning could go a long way.

With the club, Phil was training us and we would do an hour, split equally into fitness and work with the ball.

Before Joe got involved, a Limerick training session was generally around 30 minutes. You'd get a ball, split into backs and forwards and puck around for a while. Then you would have a bit of target practice, a few laps of the field and half a dozen sprints.

That was it.

Joe bumped it up to an hour and a half straight away.

It took a while to adjust, but nobody complained. We didn't really have anything else to do anyway. We loved it. Most of us had no cars, so a taxi would pick us up at our front doors, then drop us back afterwards.

We thought we were VIPs.

WE ENDED UP reaching five league finals in-a-row.

In the 1970-71 league final, we played Tipp in Cork, a huge occasion. It was a tight game, but they pulled away from us in the second-half. We reeled them in, and in the dying minute I got a free down near the corner flag.

It was one of the first real pressure frees I had taken for the county, but my confidence was growing all the time. It was a tight angle, but I sized it up and said I'd go for the score. We beat them by a point, 3-12 to 3-11.

It was the first national title a Limerick team had won since the 1947 league. We paraded the cup around the town on the Monday night, and it was striking to see so many people, particularly older people, with tears in their eyes.

We started off down at the train station and worked our way around the town, before coming back down O'Connell Street. Every street was thronged. I started to get even more of an appreciation of what it meant to represent Limerick.

The whole experience blew my mind.

We really wanted to make a mark in the championship, but it was still proving a hurdle too high for us. We beat Clare in the first round of Munster after a replay, but Cork beat us in Thurles the next day out. Still, we had made real progress that year.

We knew we had a solid foundation to build on.

I WAS MEANT to play for a Munster team in an interprovincial game on St Patrick's Day in 1971. It was a glorious day as we drove up. One of those days where people were stopping on the side of the road for picnics, just to enjoy the weather for a moment on the long drive.

I had no sense of direction at all, so I wasn't too sure how we'd get to Croke Park but I knew if I aimed for Dublin we'd get there somehow.

So, we got to Dublin anyway, but got badly held up in traffic.

We looked into the next lane and saw Mick Herbert sitting in the back of a taxi across the road. Mick had hurled for Limerick in a past life, and was a great friend of Mary's family. At that stage he was a TD, so we copped he was headed for Croke Park, and we decided to follow his taxi.

We ended up in Dáil Éireann, and I was so late to the match that I wasn't able to tog out.

THAT SUMMER WE beat Waterford in the Munster quarter-finals down in Cork, and it was another good day for myself. I scored 1-5, and Éamonn scored 1-1 too. Next we played Cork, and Joe really had us pumped for it. We had a bad record against Cork, but because of Joe we went into the game fully believing in ourselves. There are moments of that game that I can remember crystal clear. I was playing centre-forward, and Éamonn was in midfield. A ball was picked out between Éamonn and Gerald McCarthy, and when a ball like that dropped between two players like that, you would expect to see lumps of ash flying through the air.

Instead, Éamonn just pulled on it first time in the air, and it dropped perfectly to me. I was able to make some room for myself and strike for a goal.

I'll never forget that moment.

I'm still not sure if Éamonn meant it, because that ball could have gone anywhere, but for the sake of the story we'll say it was a brilliant pass. It set us on our way to our first win against Cork in the championship since 1940.

I ended up scoring 1-8 that day, and we won 2-16 to 2-14.

We were breaking a lot of milestones now, and it was all down to Joe McGrath's work. The talent had always been there, but he was helping us maximise our potential. The final was against Tipp in Killarney, and even though we played pretty well and scored 3-18, they beat us by a point.

It was heartbreaking.

We had a goal disallowed, and we had a bit of a feeling that for some reason or another, we never got the rub of the green when we played in Killarney. Frank Murphy, who went on to become secretary of the Cork county board, was referee that day. None of us could figure out why the goal was crossed out. I was the second last man to hit the ball, and before Willie Moore finished it to the net Murphy blew for a free in.

Nobody had fouled me. We were two points down at the time so the goal would have put us a point ahead. We were running out of time. We scored the point from the free, then got another.

The game got very scrappy then, as we both wanted to avoid a draw and get the win. John Flanagan got on the ball for Tipp, and he was about to strike it when our corner-back, Anthony O'Brien hit him a belt of a shoulder.

Flanagan had been kind of stumbling when he collected the ball, but the shoulder from Anthony actually straightened him out a bit.

He drove the ball over the bar, and we lost by a point.

How unlucky can you get? We all knew that we should've won that game. I still think that that was the best Limerick team I ever played on. To be fair Tipp were hardly a bad side either. Babs Keating was at his best that day, and scored 3-4. If a fella scores that much, his team will come out on top 99 times out of 100. We dusted ourselves down and told ourselves we would come back stronger next year.

We reached the league final again in 1972, but Cork beat us in Thurles. We had been playing well though, and our improvement over the last few years wasn't going unnoticed. We ended up getting to go and play in a mini-tournament in London, where we played an exhibition game against Tipp, who were the All-Ireland champions, in Wembley.

It was a mad experience. There were about 30,000 at the game, 99% of whom were Irish. The night before, we met up with the Tipp lads. Given the nature of the game, you wouldn't be too concerned about minding yourself for the match.

It wasn't exactly stretching sessions and an early night. The pints started flowing. Around midnight, poor Joe McGrath walked in and saw the scene.

He came over to me and asked me to get the lads organised and up to bed. I told him that was no problem, we'd head up right away, knowing that we were going nowhere for a while yet. Just as Joe turned and went to leave,

Leonard Enright came around the corner with a massive tray of pints.

Joe just looked him up and down and gave up the fight, accepting that it was a lost cause. He didn't even mention it the next day, with the dressing-room stinking of drink.

We had a great night socialising with the Tipp boys. That's only a tiny snapshot of what the craic could be like within the group. I think the fact that we could do that helped make playing so enjoyable. There was such a bond between us, and we were able to go and unwind as a group.

Now there is so much pressure attached with playing for your county. Players are scrutinised so much, and can go nowhere without someone knowing about it. Especially with social media. Supporters know what half of the lads are having for dinner during the week.

No-one knew the craic in Wembley until we came back and told them ourselves. Plenty of people didn't fully believe us.

I remember telling the story about us all diving into a big pool in the dressing-room after the game, and people would be rolling their eyes. Sure, we didn't even have showers in half the grounds here.

Those things opened our eyes a bit.

You hop on a short plane trip and you see a different world altogether. Croke Park was big, but Wembley was on another level.

Everything was so grand.

Then you come back and head off for a Munster championship game in Ennis, where they had no dressing-rooms. We would get togged out in the Queens Hotel, then walk across the road in our gear to play the match. It was the same in Cork, before the Athletic Grounds became Páirc Uí Chaoimh in 1976. We used to get changed into our gear in the Victoria Hotel, which was a fair walk from the stadium. Then we would drive up the road in our kit. After the game, the traffic would be too bad to drive, so we generally just walked back with all the supporters, trudging along in the crowd in our dirty gear.

That wasn't a pleasant place to be if things hadn't gone your way, which they often didn't in Cork. If it was a bad loss, or you played particularly poorly, some lads would just bundle into the cars and hang around waiting for the traffic to die down.

It was a safer option than taking the abuse in the street.

« CHAPTER 16 »

SOME PEOPLE WERE talking us up as favourites for the Munster championship in 1972. We headed down to Ennis to play Clare in the Munster semi-final, and it was an absolute disaster of a day for us.

I'm always wary of how difficult it is to beat Clare in Ennis, and that was even truer then than it is now. The pitch was nowhere near the standard of most other pitches, so that was straight away a big advantage to them. You really felt like you were in enemy territory. Nothing went right for us, and I had found it hard to get into the game myself.

I didn't start the game because I was carrying a shoulder injury.

I wasn't too debilitated, but we thought we would win so I was left on the bench as a precaution. I only scored two points when I came on, and we lost 3-10 to 2-7. Cork wasn't a nice place to be on the losing side, but Clare was just as bad.

That was it for another year. We were out of the championship without even getting to give a proper account of ourselves.

I was mad as hell.

THAT DEFEAT WAS enough to cause rumblings in the county, and some wanted Joe McGrath's head. As far as the players were concerned that was all nonsense, as we knew how much he had brought to the table.

Joe was a decent, honest man and only wanted the best for us.

Some couldn't see that and he was removed as manager. Five of the players who were instigators in bringing Joe in, Bernie Hartigan, Éamonn Grimes, Pat Hartigan, Joe McKenna and Jim Hogan, went on strike. There was a four-man committee formed to pick a new set-up.

Jackie Power and Dick Stokes, both All-Ireland winners in 1940, were both involved in that. So, the five lads went on strike anyway, but the rest of us decided that we were here to hurl, regardless of who was manager. Of course, the strike wasn't a nice thing to happen, but the one good thing that came out of it was that we unearthed three good players in their place. Frankie Nolan, Liam Donoghue, and Seamus Horgan, the goalkeeper, all had to step up to fill in for the lads.

That whole saga rumbled on for a long time.

We went through the league without those five lads, and only lost one match. Naturally enough that made the county board feel justified in their decision to get rid of Joe. Then we played Wexford in the league final, and at that stage the five lads, thanks to a few approaches from some of the players, including myself, agreed to come back into the fold.

I'm sure the fact that we were winning without them helped our case. So, we had our five lads back and went into the league final feeling really confident in what we were doing.

You can imagine the reaction back home after we lost, and lost well, to Wexford, 4-13 to 3-7. The damage went beyond that defeat too, as we lost some important personnel that day. Mickey Graham broke his leg and Tim O'Donnell also got a bad injury, so we were down two very good players for the championship. They were a big loss for us.

There was a bit of tension heading into the Munster championship. We had really improved as a group but we were aware that we hadn't delivered in Munster.

We were back in Thurles.

The rivalry with Clare was massive at that time. Even on a personal level, my brother-in-law, Jackie Gorman was playing for them. Although we won by a couple of points, we knew we were fortunate to come through the game.

Seamus Horgan made a brilliant save from Noel Casey, which I can still picture as clear as day. If that had gone in, I don't think I'd be writing this book at all. So, thanks for that Seamus.

That put us in a Munster final against Tipp, back in Thurles again. It was their home stadium obviously, but I didn't mind.

I loved Thurles.

It was the best surface around, so it always gave you the best chance to perform. The game was played on a scorching hot day in late July. It was over 30 degrees, with more than 30,000 people piled into the ground. There wasn't much between ourselves and Tipp at that stage, and I don't imagine too many people would have felt that there was a clear favourite to win the game.

Éamonn Cregan's brother, Mickey was the new trainer, and that was proving to be an added obstacle off the pitch. Lads were blaming Eamon, saying he was behind getting rid of Joe, which he wasn't. Regardless of who was right or who was wrong, the episode had put more pressure on us to deliver. If we lost again, it would be like the players were the problem.

I found Mickey to be a great trainer. If he said it, you'd do it. One of his biggest strengths was that he was great with bringing the lads that were lagging behind up to speed as well. We had a really good, strong and fit panel going into the game.

Éamonn played corner-forward against Tipp, and I was pushed back into midfield. The semi-final against Clare had been my first time playing in the middle for Limerick, and I did well enough that I was picked there again with Éamonn Grimes against Tipp.

It was nip and tuck to start with, but the game eventually opened up. It turned into a strange game. We were scoring goals for fun but were struggling for points, and they had the opposite problem.

We were a point up near the end, and Tom Ryan came in and gave away a silly free. It was a needless late tackle after his man had struck the ball, so the free was taken from where the ball landed. Francis Loughnane drove it over the bar to level the game with hardly any time left to play.

There was a throw-in then about 60 yards out, and Liam O'Donoghue, a fairly light lad, was going to go in for it against Len Gaynor, who wouldn't spare you, to put it politely. I felt it was a bit of a mismatch so I went in for it instead. I caught the ball, passed it out to Frankie Nolan, he moved it on to Éamonn Grimes, Eamonn had a shot and the goalie blocked it out for a 70.

Sean Foley was our designated man to take the 70, but Jackie Power called me out to take it. I duly obliged. I lined it up, and I did feel the pressure of the shot. The game was practically up, and I knew this would be it.

I took a deep breath, and then hit it as hard as I could.

I looked up and watched it sail over the bar.

Game over. A feeling of joy, mixed with relief, poured over me. Our first Munster title in 18 years. We watched the match back in Mickey Cregan's house that night, and when I scored the point the camera caught me doing a highland fling in the middle of the pitch. 'Jaysus,' said Mickey. 'That's the fastest you moved all day Bennis.'

Mickey had no problem in regularly reminding me that I was no speed merchant.

To this day I still meet a lot of Tipperary fellas who are happy to tell me that the ball went wide. I was at a wedding in the K Club about 10 years ago, and early enough in the night I got chatting to a couple of people who were at the game. They were all Tipp lads and had been in the stand behind the goal, and after a while they started joking that the ball had gone a few inches wide. I bumped into the game around midnight, when a few pints had been taken, and they had now decided that it was in fact about six yards wide.

By breakfast the ball was almost out towards the corner flag.

After winning the Munster final we played London in the All-Ireland semi-final. London had beaten Galway, which was naturally a huge shock. Playing London was a bit of a novelty for us, and Ned Rae was marking his brother on the London team.

The county board decided to take that match down to Ennis, which was a mad decision in our eyes because it suited London with the bad pitch. We won 1-15 to 0-7 eventually but it was touch and go for a while.

After that the All-Ireland final madness began.

FOR ME, AS I've already explained in the prologue to this book, the birth and uncertainty over the health of our first born, Dickie was all that was on my mind as the game got closer. For the remainder of the squad, and for everyone else in the county, there was excitement mixed with pandemonium.

In some respects, for me, it was almost a relief to start the game and get it over with as fast as possible,

OUT ON THE pitch, finally, we didn't really do much of a warm-up.

We just pucked the ball around a bit. It's not like nowadays, when teams have elaborate warm-up drills which can make you tired even looking at them.

It was an awful wet day.

Kilkenny were short a few important players, and there was a big thing made of that, but we were also short Mickey Graham and Jim O'Donnell.

And it was still a fine Kilkenny team. Fan Larkin, Nicky Orr, Frank Cummins, Chunky O'Brien, Pat Delaney, Claus Dunne were all present and correct... Brian Cody was just 19 at the time but was already a leader on that team. He started at wing-back, taking most of their defensive frees.

Our selectors came up with the bold idea of playing Éamonn Cregan at centre-back, where he played with his club anyway, to mark Pat Delaney.

Éamonn had been playing corner-forward up to that point, but in truth, he could play anywhere. It turned out to be a brilliant move.

The very first throw-in, I went in with Chunky O'Brien, both of us pulled and Chunky went down. I was accused of knocking him out and whatever, which I maybe would have done on a different occasion, but it was the farthest thought from my mind in this particular instance. He gave me plenty of good craic about it down the line after the game.

Cregan started really well at half-back and fielded a huge amount of high ball. You could tell early on that he was going to have a massive say on how the result went. Delaney was hardly getting a sniff.

Kilkenny got the opening goal midway through the first-half.

Mick Brennan was fouled while baring down on goal as Willie Moore and Jim O'Brien both tackled him. Claus Dunne took the free, with about six of us on the line. His shot was blocked, as was the rebound, but Delaney found the net on the second rebound.

That put them 1-3 to 0-5 up after 20 minutes.

The goal gave them a good bit of momentum. They cleared the next few balls and a few things didn't fall our way. Frankie Nolan hit the post from an angle where he'd usually score.

I had a couple of frees early on.

In the Munster final I had gone for goal from the start, but it hadn't really worked so I was happy enough to just take my points this time. You don't want to leave any scores behind in an All-Ireland final.

I struck a free around 25 minutes in that brought us within a point.

I got another a couple of minutes later, about 50 yards out this time, and that brought us level. At that stage I had three points to my name and was feeling good about my striking. I had connected well with a few balls, and on a wet day it's always good to get a feel for things nice and early.

The next free was right under the posts, following a foul after I had dropped a free in from about 70 yards, and that put us back in the lead. I had scored the last three scores of the game, all from frees.

AT THAT STAGE, it felt like Kilkenny couldn't get to grips with us. Cregan was just winning ball after ball in our half-back line. I got another couple of frees, and by the time I popped over my sixth from the 21-yard line, we led 0-10 to 1-6.

In general play, I was mainly just trying to win ball and drop it in for our forwards. You'd always back the lads to get the better of their marker and make something of it. I dropped one in for Ned Rea, our full-forward, and he beat his man and fired over to give us a two point lead.

We traded a couple more points, and we were two ahead at half-time.

The dressing-room was calm.

We knew we were going well, but we also knew we could improve, and that Kilkenny wouldn't need much of an invitation to take control.

We moved things around a bit for the second-half. Éamonn Grimes was pushed into the half-forward line and Bernie Hartigan came out beside me in midfield.

Kilkenny started to come back into it a bit and pulled our lead back. Mick Crotty then had a great goal chance for Kilkenny from point blank, but somehow Séamus Horgan managed to block it, and it flicked up over the bar.

It put them one point ahead, but if they had got the goal at that stage and moved three clear, who knows what would have happened?

It was a massive moment in the game.

Neither team had been more than two points clear at any stage, and we had been level seven times. Still, I long had the sense it was going to go our way, and I wasn't the only one. At one stage when the play stopped dead and we were a point down, this huge chant of 'LIMERICK… LIMERICK' rang around the stadium.

The supporters, drenched in the stands, were full of belief.

Shortly afterwards, I won a ball and was fouled as I soloed in towards the goal. From the free we were level again.

The place was rocking now.

Liam O'Donoghue won the puck-out, and charged back in towards the Kilkenny defence. He played in Frankie Nolan, who was absolutely clattered as he tried to release a shot. The ball broke free just in front of the goal, and somehow, in the middle of an absolute mess of bodies, Mossie Dowling managed to whip the ball into the net.

Half the crowd didn't have a clue who scored it.

That put us up, 1-13 to 1-10 with 10 minutes played in the second-half.

Bernie Hartigan struck a fine point to put us four up!

You could barely hear the man beside you breathe now. As Hartigan jogged back out the pitch, Éamonn Grimes gave him a pat on the arse with his hurley.

We knew we were flying it.

Four points was the biggest lead of the day, but we also knew that Kilkenny were never dead. In the previous All-Ireland final, in 1972, they had been trailing Cork by eight points with less than 15 minutes to play, but went on to win by seven.

We knew that if we managed to get our foot on Kilkenny's throat, we had to finish the job. To this day, that hasn't changed.

We won the next puck-out again and drove forward but had a goal disallowed for a foul on the goalkeeper. And while things were going well for me from frees, Kilkenny weren't missing any chances themselves. At the other end, Claus Dunne scored his sixth free from six attempts.

I WAS EAGER to try to put the game to bed.

I went for goal from a free on the 21 yard line, despite the fact Kilkenny had about eight bodies on the line. I struck it low, and although Ned O'Donoghue was right in on top of the rebound it was booted clear to safety.

Those are the moments that can come back to haunt you.

I hoped it wouldn't cost us. I found myself in an identical situation a few minutes later, but took the safe option and stuck it over.

There was a slight delay in getting another sliothar as the ball had been lost to the crowd in the Canal End. I saw later on the television coverage, Michael O'Hehir joked that I had probably sent it up to one of my 'six or seven brothers' in the crowd on purpose.

After some scrappy play around the middle the ball broke to me and I made off towards the right hand side of the pitch. I was able to make enough room to let fly for the posts, and scored my first point of the day from play. Éamonn Grimes got the next and we were five up midway through the second-half.

It felt like chaos after that. Kilkenny started going for goals, dropping balls down around the square, and we had to defend like dogs under the pelting rain.

I was exhausted.

The decision to shift Éamonn Grimes up the pitch was working well, and he hit a great point over his left shoulder to move us five up, but still we couldn't just kill Kilkenny off. Mossie Dowling forced a great save from Noel Skehan, and Skehan collected the loose ball and went charging away up the field, but his clearance broke down around our full-back line.

The ball eventually found its way back to me, with a decent amount of space on the half-way line. From almost exactly the centre point of the pitch, I was able to take a touch, steady myself and take aim.

With that score we were six up with just over five minutes to play, and I finally felt we had them. We were hurling too well to let them back into it.

I even allowed myself a little fist pump as I got back into position, which I also later found out was picked up by the cameras.

Mossie followed up with a fine score, striking the ball beautifully as it bobbled on the ground after he was initially hooked. It was the type of score a winning team gets in the final few minutes.

Everything was clicking for us.

Next up was Frankie Nolan from a tight angle out towards the right corner. We had hit the last four scores. Kilkenny couldn't cope with us.

We were eight points up with four to play, and what I really loved was that we didn't let up. We kept going for more. If anything, the sight of the Limerick fans getting ready to burst out onto the pitch was only spurring us on. We were loving every minute of it.

Of course, Kilkenny didn't throw in the towel either.

We hit a couple of wides in between Kilkenny attacks breaking down. Liam O'Brien eventually nailed a point for them, but as it sailed over the bar there was already a huge group of Limerick supporters piled around the goal, waiting for that final whistle.

They edged towards the pitch, inch by inch.

And as soon as the puck out was taken the ref blew his whistle.

I'd say he blew it about a half a minute early as some supporters were barely able to keep off the field.

That was that.

1-21 to 1-14.

Limerick's first All-Ireland since 1940.

A 33-year wait ended.

WITHIN SECONDS WE were swarmed. I'd never felt such joy in all my life. In truth I was probably a bit relieved as well. I was happy with my contribution on a day when anything could have happened.

I finished with 10 points, two from play. With the whole build-up to the game being so disrupted, and the wet day, it was quite remarkable that things worked out so well on the pitch.

Those moments immediately after full-time are like nothing else. Just like that, you're all heroes. Whatever way your hurling career goes, you'll always have that little piece of history to look back on. The scenes with our supporters were priceless, with the green dye from their paper hats running down their faces.

It felt like the purest form of absolute joy.

After the madness of the celebrations in the dressing-room we went back to the Skylon Hotel. That couple of hours flew by.

You didn't really book tickets for the post-match reception back then, so anyone that was late wasn't let in. You had to stay away from the entrance because anytime you walked past there would be lads shouting in at you… 'Richie… 'tis myself, get me in will you?'

Some of them you would know, but there would be just as many who you didn't have a clue who they were.

I can still remember it so clearly, one of the happiest nights of my life.

I wouldn't say we even saw our bedrooms at all. There was nothing that stood out about the night, no wild stories or anything like that, just the group of us sitting around reminiscing, the sense of relief making the pints taste all the sweeter. It was a wonderful time with a wonderful group of teammates.

We had made the county proud, and we knew it. There were a lot of similarities with the 2018 All-Ireland win actually. On both occasions, Limerick teams came from slightly left-field to end a famine in the county.

The following day there was a reception for both teams at Leopardstown Racecourse, where they showed a replay of the game. It was a bit of a strange experience, and unsurprisingly it didn't last for too many more years. It must have been hell for the losing team.

The wives and girlfriends all came too, and all evening they were doing that thing that so many women do on nights out, and going to the bathrooms in packs. After a few drinks a bit of confusion kicked in, so much so that one group of women ended up going into the gents toilets, and not realising it. Instead of acknowledging their mistake, they just decided to claim the gents as their own and refused to let any men in, leaving many of us to be a bit creative in what could be classified as a toilet for the rest of the evening.

We came home that night.

The train came into Castleconnell. From there we hopped into an open-topped trailer. We stopped in for a drink in a few good GAA pubs on the way before getting to the reception at Arthur's Quay.

There must have been 60,000 or 70,000 people there. I could hardly believe my eyes.

We were on top of the world.

IN THOSE FEW days I thought a lot about how far I had come myself as a hurler. I had worked hard on improving my game, and I was getting the benefits on the pitch.

There was one little tip that always stuck with me, and made one of the most significant differences to my contribution with the team. I used to spend a lot of time practicing my free-taking. At that time the ridge on the sliotar would be almost as thick as your finger.

I remember being up in the field practicing one night. At the time I was struggling with my consistency from frees. My biggest problem with frees was managing to get the ball up right. There was a chap up in the field making his way home from the pub, and he saw me out there on my own taking shots, and struggling a bit to get enough height on the sliotar.

He watched me going through my routine for a bit, and I didn't take too much notice of him. After a while he strolled over to me, and I could smell the drink off him before I heard him. When taking frees, I used to always roll the ball up the hurley, rather than poke it up. He told me to place the ball in a way that when I rolled it up and struck it, I never made contact with the ridge of the sliotar.

I never looked back. Sometimes the most valuable advice can come from the most unexpected of sources. His little input ended up having a big say in some important games for Limerick down the years, not least the eight frees I scored against Kilkenny.

WHEN THE BEDLAM started to die down, it was back into the clubs. We didn't do much in Patrickswell that year.

In 1974 then it all started again.

Despite being reigning champions I don't recall feeling under massive pressure to win again. Everybody knows how hard it is to go back-to-back – just look at Tipp – so I think there was an element of understanding amongst the Limerick public that to defend the Liam MacCarthy would be a really exceptional achievement.

That said, there was obviously confidence.

We knew we could beat anyone, and we knew that if things went our way we had every chance of being right back in the mix again.

We made a good start to our league campaign. We beat Clare in Ennis and drew with Kilkenny at the Gaelic Grounds in our first two games.

We also beat Galway, Waterford and Wexford, before a draw with Cork.

Out last game was against Tipp in the Gaelic Grounds. I got a 21-yard free when we were five points up. It was another awful wet day, and I didn't properly rise the ball. The ball was cleared, and Cork ended up scoring two goals.

We lost by a point. If I'd have driven that free we would have won. We got to the final anyway, where again Cork beat us, and beat us well, 6-15 to 1-12.

In the Munster semi-final of the 1974 All-Ireland championship we played Waterford, and beat them down in Thurles. I scored 1-6. That set us up for a final with Clare.

The week before the game, Clare were playing Waterford in the Munster under-21 final in Thurles. I went down to the game with Jackie Gorman, my brother-in-law who played for Clare, Mary and my sister, Joan. Clare were heavy favourites, but Waterford managed to beat them.

We hopped into the car for the drive back, with myself and Mary sitting in the back, Joan driving and Jackie in the passenger seat.

Father Harry Boland, who was training Clare at the time, saw Jackie and popped his head in as we were pulling out. 'Don't mind them Jackie… we'll beat Limerick next Sunday'. He nearly died when he looked back and saw me smiling back at him.

We actually beat Clare well on the day, and got to by-pass the All-Ireland semi-final because every second year you went straight through to the final.

IT WAS KILKENNY again, and we got off to a flyer.

We were seven points to one up, but conceded two goals in the space of three minutes, with Kilkenny pulling away and getting their revenge for 12 months previously. Eddie Keher put on an exhibition, scoring 1-11.

I only managed five points, and for whatever reason we never really got into the game. They were easily the better team on the day.

In 1975 we had a really poor league, and Cork beat us in the Munster final at the Gaelic Grounds. The team was starting to break apart a bit, and I think that deep down we all knew our best days were perhaps behind us.

In 1976 I started building the house I still live in, but I wasn't training as well as I should have and was dropped off the panel. I was disappointed.

I didn't actually hear that I was dropped until I read it in *The Examiner*.

It was a bit of a shock to find out that way after giving 10 years service. I never missed a match or even a training session for anything other than injury. My mother was very disappointed, and blamed everyone bar me. Yet after the initial shock settled, I knew within myself that I wasn't right. I had put on some weight and was putting so much time into the house.

The manager at the time was Kevin Long, and he was always on to me about my fitness. I had a slow approach to my hurling at the best of times. I saw myself as more of a reader of the game rather than someone who would be buzzing around trying to make things happen.

Suddenly I had a lot more free time on my hands, so I got the house built in no time.

We moved in on St Patrick's Day in 1977, and then I found myself getting back into shape again. The following year, I got called back into the panel, and was a substitute in Thurles for a Munster game against Waterford. We were by far second best on the day, and I never got brought on.

That was my last day involved with a Limerick panel.

It was a pretty underwhelming end to something which had given me some of the best days of my life. When I realised my time was up, I began to reflect on my career and that period in general for Limerick.

I'd never really given it too much thought while I was playing.

I walked away with one All-Ireland medal, one league and two Munster championships. We definitely underachieved given the talent we had.

I would put a lot of that down to the county board. They were so invested in the Gaelic Grounds at the time. They held so many Munster finals because so often, the final was Cork v Tipperary. It almost suited them to not have Limerick in the Munster final, because then they could host the game. That was certainly the impression we were under.

The money was more important than the team.

After we won the All-Ireland in 1973, a councillor named Mick Crowe came to the county board and asked them to sell the Gaelic Grounds. I was told that they were offered around three million for it, which was huge money, especially considering the state of the stadium at the time.

The proposition was to buy Mungret College for a fraction of the price, which was an old boarding school that had closed up just outside the city. It already had three or four brilliant pitches, and good quality function rooms and dressing-rooms. It even had a swimming pool, and there was added bonus of having surplus money which could be used to invest in the county.

The county board wouldn't do it.

They had no adventure in them at all. They used to drive me mad.

I felt that we achieved things in spite of them, rather than because of them. Unfortunately, that problem continued long after I stopped playing. Still, I certainly wasn't bitter when my playing career ended.

One All-Ireland medal is one more than 99 per cent of people who play the game can leave with. I felt lucky to have been involved with the county I loved.

Those years gave me some of the happiest memories of my life.

PART SIX

The Game that Smiles

PREVIOUS PAGE: Richie celebrates with his selector and nephew, Gary Kirby (top) after leading Limerick into the 2007 All-Ireland final and (below) he is joined by Imelda, Mary and Alison on the pitch.

GARY KIRBY
(Nephew, former Limerick hurler,
and Limerick selector 2006-08)

WHEN I STOPPED playing I had told Richie that I was planning on taking a break from hurling, so I was a bit surprised when he asked me to come on board with him with Limerick when Joe McKenna left.

But to be honest, I thought about it and said, 'Sure why not?'

You'd be mad to say no to an offer like that, and you couldn't turn down Richie in fairness. He's done a lot for me down through the years so I wouldn't say no to him.

With Richie being my uncle, he used to take me to matches when I was a kid. He taught me how to take frees, he'd offer little instructions on how to play the game, and he was always great in terms of giving me advice on the game.

Obviously, it's great as a kid to have an uncle who won an All-Ireland. He'd call out to the house and he'd be telling you little things, what was going on, how training was, what way they used to do things and how they would prepare for big games, the commitment that was needed.

Then when he was telling you stories about his time with Limerick we'd all be glued to every word. I'm still listening to him!

WHEN WE FIRST came on board to coach Limerick, you could see that confidence was very low within the squad. I knew there was no better man to get the confidence up than Richie.

He played a huge part in bringing the passion and the drive back into that Limerick team. Richie is a bubbly guy, and you could see that he brought a new lease of life to the whole set-up. Our main role was to try and get that confidence back into the players, and to try and get them believing in themselves again.

Richie was happy to delegate the workload.

Dave Moriarty was on top of the fitness side of things and a bit of coaching, and Richie worked with him really well. Richie would go over and put his arm around a fella and have a nice quiet word in his ear.

He was very good at the man-to-man stuff and getting the best out of a player.

His passion rubbed off on the team. He also knew his limitations. He knew that the modern game had moved on from when he played, so he would always be open to listening to other opinions.

The first season we thought we were only seeing out the year, which left us a bit limited in what we could do, whereas in the second season Richie knew he was in charge. That meant he was able to call the shots a bit more than he had been able to the year before.

He started to demand more from the players and from the county board, because he knew he was there permanently. He still didn't really change anything in terms of how the coaching set-up worked. He always trusted the lads around him to chip in and contribute.

There were times when he might have you looking at something for one match, and then the next match he'd have someone else on it, just to keep things fresh. He was very good at pin-pointing what was the right move and approach for a particular game.

Initially, we wouldn't really have felt that winning an All-Ireland was on our radar. We were primarily focused on just getting the passion back into Limerick hurling, and then bringing the guys on as far as we could.

I suppose the three games against Tipperary is really what drove the thing on.

That was probably a bit of a turning point. It gave the lads the confidence they needed. As that season went on then, we did believe that we could go further in the championship and do something special.

When I look back at that time, it's obvious that Richie brought a renewed level of confidence to the squad, but there was much more to him than that. I think the likes of Stephen Lucey and Andrew O'Shaughnessy improved as a result of being involved with Richie.

He brought that team to a new level. He certainly brought back that passion that had sort of been gone beforehand, the hurling got better and the players' knowledge of *how to play the game also improved.*

During Richie's time as manager, I felt that Limerick went from being sort of there or thereabouts to having the belief that they could actually compete with the best teams in the country.

« CHAPTER 17 »

I COULDN'T SAY that I woke up one morning and decided that I'd like to give management a go.

It was something that I just sort of fell into through the club. I had done alright managing at junior level and a few of the underage grades, but I thought that was where my management career, if you could even call it that, would end.

Phil was managing the senior team out in the club and winning trophies consistently. He wasn't going to budge, so I felt there was no room for me to step in anyway. When it came to management, I figured that one Bennis was enough. I never really bothered to chase any senior manager roles.

That isn't to say I didn't enjoy it.

I loved it, particularly in the earlier years. When you aren't married, and don't have any real family commitments, you can allow hurling to be your life. In from work, and out to the pitch every night, training with your own team and trying to help young lads improve their game. What more could a man want?

I would have bitten your hand off to manage the county team.

The idea of managing Limerick was a dream of mine, but I never really felt I had a chance of getting it. There were always other candidates who had much more experience floating around any time the county job became vacant.

I HAD A change of heart in 1996.

Tom Ryan had been over the team between 1993 and '95, and his term was up the following year. I knew that either he wouldn't look to stay on, or that the Limerick country board wouldn't keep him. Limerick had a good team, losing the 1994 and '96 finals, and had always been there or thereabouts since 1991.

I saw huge potential in them.

I thought that maybe I might have something to offer, and could help get them over the line. I let the idea fester in my mind for a few weeks and increasingly felt that maybe it was worth putting my name in the hat. I discussed it with my family, and we agreed that I'd go for it.

I put my name forward, and was beaten by one vote.

Tom Ryan got the job; not the first time I'd lost out in a head-to-head with him. It was disappointing not to get it, but it wasn't earth-shattering. I kind of felt that I wasn't what the county board wanted, and I knew they felt I didn't have the necessary experience.

At that stage, I said that was that, and I wouldn't ever apply for the job again. The experience had more or less confirmed a few doubts that had stopped me from applying previously.

From then on, I just went back to being a supporter, and a good supporter at that.

Limerick games were a real family outing. Myself, Mary, my two daughters and my sons, all out supporting the team. We went to all the games, home and away, rain or shine, league or championship.

We'd never miss a match, and over the years my daughters in particular became fanatical about Limerick hurling.

I loved watching Limerick purely as a supporter. It's a very different experience to being involved in the team. You can still enjoy the highs, but also the lows don't hurt as much. There is no time spent thinking what you could have done differently.

No 'what ifs' on your behalf.

You can watch a player do something wrong and get frustrated or annoyed, call him a fecking eejit or worse, then pack up, head home, and get on with your life. It's not as easy to live with when you're the player in question, doubting your performance or the decisions you made. Likewise, if you're a manger, thinking that you played the wrong fella or took the wrong approach.

I made the most of sitting in the stands, supporting my county and following Limerick without any feeling of pressure attached. As the years rolled by, and as Limerick rose and faded without ever delivering that elusive All-Ireland, I never would have guessed that I would one day throw myself right back into the thick of that mayhem.

THERE WAS NOTHING remarkable about the day either.

Limerick were heading to Ennis to play Clare in a play-off. Joe McKenna was the Limerick manager, and was doing a grand job. The previous year he had taken Limerick to a league semi-final, where they were beaten by a great Kilkenny team.

There weren't many complaints about the way he was doing things.

It quickly came apart for Joe, however. He tried a few things in a challenge match against Dublin, which basically involved shifting the team around a bit, and it had come up trumps. He played that same set-up against Clare in the play-off game and it didn't work. They got a right beating.

It wasn't pleasant to watch.

We were sitting in the stand as usual, and a lady turned back around towards us near the end of the game and shouted up at me.

It wasn't unusual for that to happen.

'You should take over Richie!'

I told her there wasn't a hope in hell. I meant it too. I went home and thought nothing of it. I was just recovering from my dance with septicemia at the time. Inter-county management wasn't recommended on any of the recovery programmes I had seen.

Hurling was the least of my concerns.

The following Wednesday I was out supervising a job on a septic tank, and got a call from a friend of mine, PJ Guinane around lunchtime. He'd often ring up for an auld chat about the match, so again, nothing new there.

McKenna had resigned the day after the Clare game.

'Would you not take over, Richie?'

Jokingly, I said I would… if the money was right.

He asked again. 'Would you though?'

'Ah, I would… if they were stuck,' I replied.

I wasn't thinking seriously about it at all. As far as I was concerned, this was just a casual chat between two friends. That was that, and I went on with my day.

The phone rang again at around 6.0 pm.

This time it was the chairman of the county board. He certainly wasn't one for ringing up to chat about the game. He sounded like a man in a hurry. It turned out PJ had rung him up after our earlier conversation and told him I was keen to take the job.

Limerick were back out the following Sunday, and they didn't have a manager. He told me the job was mine, if I wanted it. At first I thought he was winding me up. He told me he was being honest with me, and asked again if I would take it?

I told him what I had told PJ earlier.

'If you really are stuck… then I'll do it,' I said.

'We are!'

You wouldn't have called it a ringing endorsement. The next step was to meet up and discuss things properly. He wanted to meet somewhere where we wouldn't be spotted, in case either party had a change of heart.

A location was set, and before I knew it I was hopping into a car to go and discuss getting my dream job.

I was sitting in his car in the carpark of the Kilmurray Lodge.

Less than an hour had passed since taking the chairman's call.

I WAS TOLD that Tony Hickey, who was managing the under-21 team, would help me out. That was fine by me. I told him I needed to ask 'the boss' first.

This was a big decision, and Mary had been my guiding light all my life.

I knew that if she said to go for it, then it was the right thing to do. If she had any reservations or didn't think that the timing was right, then I'd have trusted her on that too, one hundred percent.

I went home and told her the situation.

She just laughed. This was only a couple of years after I had been on death's door, told to take it easy, and now here I was looking to step back into the ring and take on the biggest challenge of my life.

She had her reservations, but she also knew what it meant to me.

I'm sure it had hurt her to see me lose so much of my life after my illness. I was dying to get involved in something again, and this was only going to be a short-term arrangement. I knew what my doctor would say, but my opinion was that things like that energise you.

I was mad to do it.

My two daughters were there too and they were much more excited by the idea than Mary was. It didn't take long for us all to agree that I should be the next Limerick hurling manager.

The following day I called into my nephew, Gary Kirby and explained the whole situation again. He was just as surprised as anyone. I wanted him to come on board with me, but he had absolutely no interest.

There was no convincing him.

I decided that was fair enough, as it is a massive commitment. I was disappointed, but I fully understood his decision.

An hour later he rang me and said that he'd do it.

One down. Then I rang up Bernie Hartigan and got him in. Tony brought in Ger Connell. Ger was the jersey man. He drove the van around and did countless other jobs that I still probably don't know about. Ger was a brilliant operator, which is why he's still there working with Limerick now.

Just like that, our little backroom team was complete.

Now it was time to focus on the hurling.

First up, Offaly in Tullamore.

OUR FIRST NIGHT training together was a Wednesday night, and I can admit that I was bold enough with the players. I was the new man in charge, and I knew that I was only going to be there for two matches.

I had decided that I didn't give a dog's dinner about anything and I would just go in and lay down the law.

I didn't need to care what they thought about me.

I also wasn't going to try and revolutionise the way they played across two matches, so the session was all very traditional. I got them to do a bit of ground hurling, and you would swear that half of them had never hit a ball on the ground in their lives.

They were absolutely disastrous at it.

There was no point continuing with it, so I pulled the plug on it and just got them to play a match instead. I didn't feel there was any real point in getting them to do any drills or anything like that. I just needed to get a good look at them playing before the Offaly game. We were on a tight schedule.

Dave Mahedy was the trainer under Joe McKenna, and he assured me they were as fit as they needed to be. We also brought in Pat Murnan, who had won a minor All-Ireland in 1984, to do some training with them. From the little bit I saw of the lads, I was happy enough, although I hadn't had enough time to form a real opinion of what the expectation should be.

I didn't think about any sort of long-term plan. I just wanted to get the lads through these two matches and come out the other side in decent enough shape.

The Offaly game arrived quickly.

You could tell the interest in the team was fading. There wasn't a great Limerick crowd at the game. We didn't start well, and the few supporters that made the journey down were probably regretting their decision. We found ourselves six points down with about seven or eight minutes to go before half-time.

Offaly were all over us.

The game was rapidly getting away from us, so we decided that we needed to make some moves. We brought off some established fellas, who wouldn't have been too used to coming off in games. It was clear that they weren't best pleased.

I was getting the impression that some of those lads more or less did what they liked in the previous set-up. I had the luxury of knowing that we had nothing to lose, so didn't need to keep anyone onside.

About five minutes before half-time Offaly hit the bar.

They would have moved 10 points clear if they scored that goal. As it happened, we went back down the field, scored a goal ourselves, and pulled it level by half-time.

The dressing-room was absolutely buzzing.

The lads could sense that we had all the momentum now, and they were dying to get back out there. It was wonderful to see. We went out and hurled them off the pitch in the second-half. Everything went right for us. We hurled really well and won by 10 points.

That second-half performance reaffirmed my own belief in the group. Any short term thinking I had restricted myself to went out the window. I was convinced that the potential was there and that they could achieve something special. We had only one night of training before that game, so I hadn't had the time to make any real judgements on lads.

I only knew their talent from following them so closely as a supporter.

There were a few things that I felt needed to change.

Stephen Lucey had been used at centre-forward, while TJ Ryan was in at full-back. I felt both were out of position, so I swapped them around.

We played Dublin next, and beat them by six points.

It was a good result, but we were lucky to get the win. That was a good Dublin team. Their manager, Tommy Naughton was an absolute gentleman and was very good to us in terms of challenge games afterwards.

Beating Dublin put us into the All-Ireland quarter-finals. I don't think any of us expected to be there. I certainly hadn't when I took the job.

This was the point when things started to get interesting.

« CHAPTER 18 »

THERE WAS A drink culture associated with the team around that time.

I didn't know much about it myself, but you would always hear little rumours. The night after the Dublin game I went up to the Woodfield Hotel, just across the road from the Gaelic Grounds, for a meal.

I was happy as Larry after beating Dublin, so went straight up to the bar for a pint. Gary came up to me and said it wasn't a good look, because of the rumours about the team. He told me to leave it behind me.

I paid the barman, turned around and walked away.

THE BAR WAS busy so I'm sure it didn't go to waste. Gary felt that if I brought down a drink, it might have been seen as giving the lads the green light. I hadn't even thought about it. A bit of me was still in supporter mode.

Reaching the quarter-finals gave the lads real purpose when we went back training. We were playing Cork, so automatically the lads were confident. The summer was opening up in front of us.

Dave Moriarty became our full-time trainer. He had worked with the Limerick football team and they had reached two Munster finals. We had him in in time for the Cork game, but we didn't do a huge amount of training because the lads were all in good enough shape anyway. In the two weeks before playing Cork, we did three nights training each week.

One session on Sunday and two midweek.

The game was set for Thurles. Of course, we were given no hope given our track record earlier in the championship. I went into the game with the mindset that it was my last match as manager. I pulled out all the stops, and put a fair bit of pressure on the players.

That included telling them some home truths.

I could see that they were taken aback by some of the things I was telling them, which was surprising. I got the impression that it been some time since they last received a good rollicking. They needed it if we were going to go any further.

I told the lads that I was aware of the rumours of a bit of a drink culture, but I didn't know for sure about anything. I didn't accuse anybody of anything. I just told the lads that if something was going on, it had to stop. Or we would get nowhere as a team.

CORK WERE GOOD, and went five or six points up.

They couldn't shake us off though. We kept hanging in there, and at the start of the second-half we pulled it back to just one point.

Brian Geary caught a ball, and the referee blew a free against him at a time when all the momentum was with us. There was about five minutes left to play.

To this day I think it should have been a free for us, but that's sport. Ben O'Connor drove the free over and Cork were two points clear, with time nearly up. We had been doing well, and although we were chasing the game, we had never really faded in the second-half.

I knew we were still alive.

The place was going mad. I'd heard people say that you can barely hear yourself think in that environment, and it's true. Mike O'Brien, who was in midfield, got a ball and soloed in towards goal. Amidst all the noise and confusion, Mike thought that there was only a point in the game. He stuck it over the bar, thinking he had levelled the match.

The ref blew it up and we lost by a point.

Well fuck it anyway!

That was my first thought.

My second thought was that we had put in a great performance. I was hugely proud of the lads.

After that game, I got great claps coming off the field.

I met a few supporters afterwards and sure everyone thought I was a great fella. A few months ago, we could barely get a crowd out to watch a qualifier against Offaly. Now we should have at least drawn an All-Ireland quarter-final against Cork.

That was supposed to be me clocking off.

My term as manager was over as I only had come in to see out the championship. But I had loved every minute of it.

I'd got the bug.

THE JOB WAS up for election, and I said I'd put my name forward. I was by no means a shoo-in. There were five or six others who also wanted the chance. Plenty of lads had seen the potential that I knew was there.

The job was certainly more attractive than it had been earlier that year.

I went in to do my interview, and I'd be surprised if mine wasn't the shortest of the lot. I told them that they didn't need to ask me anything.

I said they knew what I was capable of, and that I just wanted them to pick whoever they felt was the right man, whether that was me or whether it was somebody else. I knew who I was up against, and I was fairly confident that they'd go with me again.

Tom Ryan had been toying with the idea of coming back again, but pulled out at the last minute. I'd say he would have gotten it if he went for it. Éamonn Cregan also considered it before deciding against it. So, after that very brief chat, I went out for a drink.

Not long afterwards the phone rang.

I was told I had the job.

The next question was, 'How much do you want?'

I had never been paid any money for any job in the GAA in all my life. I told them I didn't want any money, and that I was happy once my expenses were covered.

I'm sure they were even happier with the arrangement than I was.

It was probably a bit naive on my behalf. In the end, it actually cost me money to be Limerick manager over the two years. That annoyed me, but I didn't lose any sleep over it.

Once I had the job officially it was time to get down to work.

I knew that the dynamics of the job would be quite different this time around. The first year I had only gotten a taste of it really. It was just a case of getting in and trying to steady the ship somewhat. This time, with a full pre-season ahead of us, I had time to actually mark out some goals and try to put my own stamp on things a bit.

I was excited about it. I felt having some bit of certainty and structure would allow us a chance to really get the best out of the lads.

We flew through pre-season. There were some tough sessions. Moriarty put the lads through their paces, but everyone really bought in to what we were doing. You could see the belief in the lads. They were dying to have a real crack at it this time.

I couldn't wait to get to training each evening.

It was a wonderful environment. There's something magical about a group all pulling in the one direction, working hard for each other.

I hadn't felt that alive in years.

The team was in great condition come the start of the league. Out first league match was against Tipperary. The league has grown into a funny competition. Different teams treat it differently. I felt that it could be as important as we wanted to make it.

Some teams would try to hold everything back for championship. There was no point in us doing that. We were too long without an All-Ireland. We hadn't even won a Munster championship since 1996.

It's a difficult balance to try strike in terms of preparing the players mentally. A good league would only serve to boost the confidence within the squad. That said, I knew that if things didn't go our way it wouldn't be the end of the world.

We were also set to play Tipperary in the Munster championship, so we got our heads together and said we would set out to put in a good performance against them in the league, as a way of setting down a marker for the bigger battles that lay ahead. Get into their heads nice and early.

Thurles was closed at the time, so the game was held in Nenagh.

I'm sure Tipp hated being moved out of their usual home ground. They were actually late to the stadium on the day. That's only a little thing, but I loved it. Beating the home team to their own stadium.

That was one early little boost.

We hurled well but couldn't pull clear. It was level with around 10 minutes left to play, but Ollie Moran scored a rocket of a goal for us. He was about 25 meters out when he struck it, but Brendan Cummins had no chance. I'd say he barely knew what had happened until he heard the net shake behind him. We pushed on from there and beat them by six points.

I was delighted with the way the lads attacked the game. The result was great, but even more pleasing was the performance.

We looked clinical and organised.

Andrew O'Shaughnessy scored 1-8, including a wonderful goal in the first-half. We kept Tipp to 16 points. I thought that us keeping a clean sheet against them was the type of thing that could really play on their minds. My confidence in the lads was increasing by the week. I had no problem in telling reporters that we'd be competing for trophies.

I could sense that the supporters were really behind us too.

They could see that the group was heading in the right direction, and in turn the lads fed off that. The belief from outside began to trickle into the group and they steadily grew in confidence.

Maybe we relaxed things a little after that.

Galway beat us comfortably in the Gaelic Grounds. We also lost to Kilkenny and Dublin before signing off with a win against Antrim. That put us into a relegation play-off with Offaly, which we won easily, 6-20 to 1-18.

Overall, I was happy with the shape we were in.

We had our big win against Tipp, and then just fine-tuned our fitness throughout the rest of the campaign. There was no shame in losing to Galway, Kilkenny and Dublin at that time of year, and the lads knew as much themselves.

In a way I was glad to get the league out of the way.

We were all mad to get going in the championship.

« CHAPTER 19 »

FINALLY, JUNE 10 arrived.

A Munster semi-final against Tipperary in the Gaelic Grounds.

Jesus, if you couldn't get excited for that, then you're in the wrong game. It had been 11 years since Limerick last won a Munster championship. Ending that drought was our target, and I knew that every single one of the lads felt it was within our capabilities.

We could give anyone a game.

Tipp got off to a flying start. John Carroll scored an early goal for them. Things got worse for us when Damien Reale was sent-off after picking up his second yellow card with just 20 minutes played. The lads needed to settle things down.

Or it was going to turn into one of those horribly long evenings for us.

Yet despite having the extra man, Tipp couldn't put the game to bed. To be fair to our lads, not a single head dropped when Damien was sent-off. They all just readjusted, knowing that if they lived with Tipp for the next 10 minutes or so then they could stay in the game. They did just that.

Heading into the last few minutes Tipp were up by three points.

Then Pat Tobin hit a wonderful goal. Ollie Moran fielded a high ball, and surrounded by Tipp players he managed to palm it out to Pat, who stuck it from a difficult angle. It was the type of goal that could win Goal of the Year in any season. A replay.

We'll take that.

The replay was set for Thurles, just six days later.

It's not only in recent years that the GAA has had problems with its calendar.

Babs Keating was Tipperary manager at the time. He decided to drop his goalkeeper, Brendan Cummins for Gerry Kennedy after the drawn game, and came in for some heat in the build-up to the replay. Our build-up was absolutely perfect. Focused and relaxed, no distractions.

Again, they were the better side for much of the match, and had moved 10 points clear by half-time. Yet over the weeks I had seen our lads develop this unbelievable trait, which wasn't something I had noticed when I was sitting in the stands as a supporter. No matter the circumstances or the situation, they never felt that a game was beyond them.

There was a real sense of calm in the dressing-room. It was just, 'Let's get back out there… and play our game'.

Ollie Moran was inspirational in the second-half, and we steadily clawed back the deficit. We were 10 points down again with about 15 minutes left to play and some Tipp supporters started heading off to beat the traffic.

We were sticking points every couple of minutes, and Tipp weren't really adding to their own tally. Maybe they had taken their foot off the gas a bit, thinking we'd throw in the towel. We were still six points down with five minutes left to play.

We'd also struck three times the amount of wides as Tipp.

The lads had it down to four points entering the last minute, and then they announced there was three added minutes to play.

We had four minutes to get four points.

Ollie Moran plucked a ball from the sky and found the posts.

Three minutes to get three scores.

Gerry Kennedy hit Benny Dunne from the puck-out. He aimed a ball towards the half-forward line, but Mark Foley cleared it out to Donal O'Grady in midfield. He found Ollie, who made no mistake again.

Having been held to one point for most of the match he'd just hit two huge points on the bounce. Two minutes to get two scores.

Tipp went long with the puck-out. Eoin Kelly ended up with the ball down in the corner but gave it away under pressure from Damien Reale.

Brian Geary sent it long.

We coughed it up but Tipp failed to clear their lines, and the ball broke to Ollie down in the right corner. He took a few steps, cut inside and scored.

One score to go, less than a minute to play.

Seamus Hickey won the puck-out and sent a booming ball back down Tipperary's throats. O'Shaugnessy won it and was fouled as he hared in on goal.

Right in front of the posts. I actually raced out towards the pitch I was so excited. Shaughs would score it in his sleep. The game was level for the fourth time.

Full-time.

We outscored them 1-9 to 0-2 in those final stages.

Tipp pulled clear at the start of extra-time. Darragh Egan struck a goal for them. Babs had substituted Lar Corbett when Tipp were looking comfortable but decided to throw him back on, and he hit an important point for them.

Shaughs missed a great goal chance but then levelled the game from a '65'.

Tipperary 2-21, Limerick 1-24.

An epic.

MYSELF AND BABS were interviewed by RTÉ on the pitch afterwards.

I threw my arm around him and told the camera that he was one of the great hurling men. I was buzzing. It had been a great evening of hurling.

I signed off by saying… 'Limerick and Tipperary has been a great hurling rivalry… and long may it last'.

I HAD MADE plans for a few different scenarios ahead of the championship, but I certainly hadn't given any thought to a trilogy against Tipp right at the start of our campaign. I was still only finding my feet as manager.

The inter-county scene that I had been involved in as a player, and the one I was now entering as a manager, were absolutely worlds apart. Even small things like going to the pool the following morning for recovery sessions, something like that would never have been on my radar. I quickly had to get up to speed with things that are now standard practice. Moriarty was brilliant with all of that.

Ice baths for the lads.

Training sessions at 7.0 am.

I was better dealing with the on-pitch stuff. For all the bells and whistles around the game, what happens on the pitch doesn't change drastically. That was the area where I really had to deliver for the team.

For the third game against Tipp, we decided to change our approach. We thrashed out various possible solutions, and Gary Kirby brought up the idea of playing a sweeper. I felt that it could work. We pulled back Kevin Tobin, a corner-forward, and kept him around the midfield area. It was only a small tweak, but it really confused Tipp. Kevin was a brilliant hurler, and excellent on the ball, so we knew that he'd be able to influence the game for us from there.

The quality of the previous two games had driven interest through the roof, and 50,000 turned up to watch the third instalment at the Gaelic Grounds. Luckily for them, it was just as mad and frantic as the first two games.

Kevin did really well in his new surroundings.

The position suited him. Niall Moran was also superb at wing forward, and hit 0-5 from play. We raced into a 0-7 to 0-1 lead after just 20 minutes, but they pulled us back level by half-time.

We both traded scores in a tight second-half, but we were slowly growing into the game as it wore on. With five minutes left Niall and his brother, Ollie really lifted things up a notch and we looked home and hosed with a three points lead. Despite the madness of the last two games, I could hardly believe what I was seeing as Tipp lifted it in the blink of an eye.

They cut it to two points.

Then one point.

And then a Seamus Butler point sent us to extra-time.

Again.

WE WERE TWO points down by the end of the first period of extra-time, with Willie Ryan scoring a goal for Tipp.

What happened next was simply exceptional from our players. Brian Geary got the first score of the second period from way out. That was his third point of the day. He was exceptional across the three games. Barry Foley ended up one-on-one at an acute angle but Gerry Kennedy made a great save. Kennedy stayed down for a bit after taking a belt of the sliothar in the midriff from point blank range.

Shaughs stuck the '65' and we were level for the seventh time.

Mark Foley won a free and jumped in the air. The Limerick crowd roared him on. We missed another decent chance during a goalmouth scramble just after that. The ball came back down the field and Foley absolutely floored Thomas Stapleton with a huge hit. Stapleton stayed down as Mark pumped his fists.

We even got the free, somehow.

Mark was having a monster of a game, 11 years on from winning his first All Star. Shaughs put us a point up. Tipp came back at us and this time Foley flattened Seamus Butler. Mark, who was 32 years of age, was popping up everywhere.

Tipp got the free this time, but it was soft. I was standing right in front of it. Eoin Kelly dropped the free short and we got it clear. The game became increasingly chaotic. I don't know how they were deciding what was a free and what wasn't, for either team.

Barry Foley gathered a ball at the second attempt with the clock in the red. Despite having three Tipp players surrounding him he managed to find Ollie Moran, and Ollie whipped it straight over the bar. We won the puck-out, but sent the ball wide.

We won the next puck out too.

Niall Moran sent it over from a huge distance. The place went absolutely bananas. Kennedy sent another big puck out down the pitch but it was swallowed up by a mass of Limerick supporters who had burst out onto the pitch. The referee had to stop the game temporarily as we told them to get back into the stands.

It was pandemonium.

Play resumed with a throw-ball in the middle of the field, but the ref blew it up about two seconds after he dropped the ball. I bear hugged Gary before we both skipped out onto the pitch.

Everywhere I turned a new set of arms threw themselves around me.

THE LIMERICK SUPPORTERS poured out of the stands and spilled out across the pitch. Those moments just soak you up and carry you along, and before you know it the chaos has died down and you're back in the dressing-room trying to remember all of the faces you saw as people of all ages wearing green jerseys swarmed around you in those mad few minutes after the final whistle.

The outpouring of emotion was extraordinary.

You'd swear we had actually won a bloody trophy! It just showed how long Limerick fans had been suffering. Looking at it coldly, we had only won a Munster semi-final. But you couldn't look at a saga like that coldly.

A Limerick team had gone toe-to-toe with a strong Tipp side for a total of four hours and 10 minutes over the course of a month, and we had won.

Despite losing a man 20 minutes into the first game.

Despite falling 10 points down by half-time in the first replay.

We had stuck at it and we had come out on top. That's all Limerick people ever want to see from their teams: a bit of desire. From a managerial point of view, I loved the fact that we were finishing games so strongly. In the second replay, we outscored Tipp 0-5 to 0-0 at the end of extra time. It was our first championship win over them in 11 years.

RTÉ asked me what I'd done with the team to transform them, and I said I had done nothing. It was all down to the players. They were truly extraordinary that day. We didn't even have to say a word to them before extra-time. They just spoke among themselves about what they needed to do.

It was great to see them celebrate after. You could hardly move out on the pitch. It was bedlam, it was brilliant, but it was exhausting.

You'd almost want a summer off after it.

Thankfully we didn't have that option, and it was time to prepare for a Munster final.

There was a great picture in the newspapers the following day of myself and Babs embracing at the end. It was just a heat-of-the-moment thing; we had been through so much over the three games that there was a sense of respect there between us.

I liked Babs.

I thought he was a good GAA man, but he's gone a little bit hard on people over the years. I was at an event before the 2018 All-Ireland final where we were both interviewed as part of a panel for a podcast, and I actually felt sorry for him.

He holds hard thoughts towards Tipp too. I had a word with him afterwards and told him that he was the only one that was suffering. He owed Tipp nothing. He won two All-Irelands with them, and three as a player.

I mean… *Bloody hell!*

I couldn't understand it. Some people just can't let go. Most people would wear that record as a badge of honour.

I HAD CHANGED my approach to managing the team for the second campaign. I had still been fairly tough on the lads during the league, but I had started to ease up for the championship.

I didn't need to be on their case anymore, because they were doing everything that was asked of them and we were going well. It hadn't been a natural approach for me anyway, so I was happy to turn down the temperature a bit. I could see that the lads were self-motivated now. The Tipperary games had cemented the belief within the group that we could achieve something this year, and that what we were doing with them was working.

We were up against Waterford in the final, and it was a bit of a novelty fixture.

There hadn't been a Limerick-Waterford Munster final for 73 years. They had managed to win their semi-final against Cork at the first attempt, so were far fresher than us. They were a great team, and had some great players in super form.

Still, we went into it confident of beating them if we got our game right. Limerick had gone hurling mad since the Tipperary games. It could be tough down here at times. It's always been a big soccer town and of course we have a huge rugby history with Munster. Despite that the hurlers have always had great support too. I really wanted to deliver a trophy for the people.

It had been far too long since we had a right celebration.

For whatever reason, things just didn't click for us against Waterford. We didn't have Damien Reale, our captain, available due to a concussion injury. Dan Shanahan scored 3-3 for them, with all three of his goals coming in the second-half.

We lost by nine points, 3-17 to 1-14.

Naturally, it was hugely disappointing, but I knew the scoreline didn't reflect the difference between the two teams. On another day we could have won the game, so I by no means lost faith in what we were doing. Barry Foley and Brian Begley had both missed good goal chances in the first-half, when the game was still tight, that they would usually take. Shanahan also scored one of his goals when we were in the middle of changing a few bodies around, when there was only four points between us. Mark Foley had just come off as a blood substitute and we had sent Mike O'Brien in.

We had got the timing of it wrong on the sideline, and Dan was left isolated inside. The lads were really down afterwards. I was talking to Justin McCarthy, the Waterford manger after the game, and I told him that if they had let us have that then we would have left the rest of the championship for them. I wouldn't have said it if I knew what was waiting down the line.

I had a brief word with our lads.

We had our dinner in almost complete silence. The way the championship worked at the time meant that both ourselves and Waterford went straight into the All-Ireland quarter-finals. The draw was made while we were on the bus back to Limerick.

We drew Clare, and a massive cheer went up.

Clare weren't going particularly well at the time, and we knew that we'd be able to beat them. Even better, the game was fixed for Croke Park.

Just like that, we were back on track.

TRAINING SESSIONS ARE a breeze when you have an achievable goal in front of you. With another group of players, the whole thing could have fallen apart after the Munster final. There was no danger of that happening with the group we had.

There wasn't a single moment on the training pitch where any of the lads wallowed in the Waterford defeat or moaned about anything we were doing.

Everyone was dying to get back out there and get going again, to show what they were capable of. They felt they hadn't given a proper reflection of themselves, and that hurt. Hurt can be a great motivator.

Everyone knew that if they put in the work, we would beat Clare in Croke Park. Trust me, for Limerick lads, it doesn't get much better than that.

The players couldn't wait to have a shot at Clare, and that enthusiasm went two ways. As a management group, we fed off the players' hunger. Likewise, they were spurred on by the belief and encouragement we showed in them. Even on the back of what had been a crushing Munster final defeat, it was a great few weeks.

I WAS SUSPENDED for the Clare game, and had to watch on from a little hut up in the Hogan Stand with a small little television in front of me.

I wasn't long-sighted, so I could barely see the game at all from where I was. I certainly couldn't see things in the detail I needed to as manager. Ger Connell was up there with me. It had been one of Ger's big ambitions to stand on the sideline in Croke Park with a Limerick team.

Seeing how disappointed he was actually distracted me slightly.

He was a brilliant character and loved Limerick hurling. He was almost crying as we walked up to take our seats before the game. He sat down, looked out onto the pitch, and quietly said to himself, 'I still haven't got to stand on that sideline'.

At half-time I decided that I had had enough. I made my way down and met a few officials who tried to stop me from getting out to the pitch. I told them that they could suspend me for life afterwards if they needed to, but that I couldn't see the match from where I was so I needed to get closer.

I was told that a television had been provided for me, but I told them I couldn't see that either. I may have exaggerated how bad my eyesight was.

A compromise was struck.

I managed to get seated right behind the team without going onto the sideline, so I got to see the second-half properly and no more suspensions came my way.

Win-win.

Poor auld Ger still didn't get out onto the sideline though.

The suspension itself was a joke anyway. I was alleged to have said something to the referee during the last of the three Tipperary games. To be fair, there have been plenty of occasions where I would have, but in this particular instance I knew that what I had said in no way warranted disciplinary action.

I had gone onto the pitch, which you are obviously not meant to do, but Mark Foley was down hurt and the game was continuing on.

I had gone on to get the referee's attention, thinking of Mark's safety. He wasn't exactly the type of fella to stay down after a hit. Earlier in the summer we had had a fella down with concussion and the game had continued on around him, so that was still fresh in my mind. I had apologised for going onto the pitch but Croke Park like to drag these things out sometimes.

I had to go up to Croke Park for a hearing.

I went up the lift to one of the boardrooms and when I went in there were about 13 or 14 fellas all sitting around this big table.

I knew a good few of them.

Most of them were retired, sitting around chatting with the few sandwiches and teas and coffees. It's a grand auld evening for them. I explained my case and apologised for going on the pitch again.

I also had a letter from Eoin Kelly, the Tipperary forward, which said that I didn't say anything deserving of a suspension. They didn't accept that. Lots of those lads like the bit of power they get at those hearings. The suspension stood.

The funny thing was, nobody who was there was able to tell me what it was I had supposedly said. I asked them straight out, because I knew what I said and that it wasn't out of line, but nobody could answer me. Some of the things that can go on with those hearings is just beyond belief.

Our own county board was also a mess at the time. The secretary had resigned, so the chairman had been left to do everything. He rang me up to inform me the suspension had been upheld, but that I had an option to appeal it. After my experience the first day, I had decided that it wasn't worth my time taking the trip back up to Dublin.

WE BEAT CLARE handy enough, as we thought we would.

Andrew O'Shaughnessy had a terrific game. On the other side of the draw, Waterford beat Cork, so we were set to meet them again in an All-Ireland semi-final.

We were delighted.

The attitude amongst our players switched to a completely new level after beating Clare. They knew that they had a real chance of making amends for the Munster final. I had never seen them so up for a game, and the most striking thing was that I didn't see one player display even the slightest hint of nerves.

I met up with the backroom team to plan out the Waterford game. We knew that their confidence was sky high, and rightly so.

They had been flying it that year. You didn't need a degree in sports management to know that Dan Shanahan was their strong point. He was scoring goals for fun that summer, and had been the difference again against Cork, scoring 2-1.

John Mullane was also playing some unreal hurling. In my opinion he was the best hurler in the country at that time. When quality forwards like that are performing to the peak of their abilities, you can't expect defenders to get the better of them on a regular basis. To a certain extent, it's more a case of damage control, while trying to score enough yourself at the other end.

That was no problem for us, we were a team that went out to attack each game. We had scored 2-65 across the three Tipperary games, and hit the 20-point mark twice. The only team to score 20 points in a Munster championship game that summer had been Tipp, against us the second time out.

Waterford's game was about goals.

Even though our defenders were playing well, we knew that we couldn't just shut out Shanahan and Mullane. We decided the more realistic option was to cut off their supply. Waterford had an excellent half-back line in Tony Browne, Ken McGrath and Darragh Fives. Their deliveries were crucial to the Waterford full-forward line.

We also knew that Seamus Hickey, who was only 19 at the time, had a great record against Mullane through underage, and would have no problem making life difficult for him on the day. Mullane even said to me afterwards that he hated the sight of Hickey, because he'd be so close to him that it constantly felt like Hickey was inside his backside pocket.

He was one of the few defenders who could live with Mullane's pace, and he'd always hurl from the front. That was the only way that you could curb Mullane's influence. Mullane was good enough that he might score a few points regardless, but in our minds that was one problem more or less looked after.

We put Sean O'Connor on Browne.

We told him that we didn't need him to score. We had enough players around him that were well capable of that. O'Connor's job was to make sure Browne never got to clear a ball with enough time to properly pick a pass. We wanted him to always feel under pressure to release the ball.

Ollie Moran on Ken McGrath was always going to be the duel of the day. Both of them were covered in blood after the game. Mike Fitzgerald was our other wing-forward, and we let him hurl away because at that stage Fives' deliveries were not as instrumental to Waterford's play as Browne's and McGrath's were.

We were also very aware that nobody was giving us a chance.

I loved that. The lads didn't need much extra motivation, but being written off so openly certainly put an extra bit of bite into them. It wasn't just that we weren't fancied, there were some people already talking about who would win in a Kilkenny v Waterford All-Ireland final?

Kilkenny had beaten Wexford comfortably the week before. The general consensus was that Waterford would also be too strong for us. The bookies heavily fancied Waterford. I thought that was mad in a two-horse race.

WE DECIDED TO go up by train on the morning of the game. I had always felt that one of Kilkenny's biggest advantages was getting to sleep in their own beds the night before an All-Ireland final. We'd have our breakfast on the train, and get the train back again that evening after the match.

Get in, get the job done, and go home.

Our lads got off to an ideal start. All the hurt from the Munster final had been pent up inside them, and they unleashed it from the moment the ball was thrown in. We hit Waterford like a hurricane.

Donal O'Grady played in Donie Ryan and we had our first goal with just over five minutes on the clock. Shaughs was lighting it up. He skinned Aidan Kearney to score our second goal 10 minutes later. Justin moved Kearney off him, giving Browne a shot before settling on Eoin Murphy.

We were 10 points up with less than 25 minutes played.

I was loving it, and made that clear to the Limerick supporters behind us in the Hogan Stand. The stadium was rocking. Waterford looked panicked. We weren't giving them a second on the ball. Any time a Waterford player got in possession, our lads would be swarming around them in seconds.

Waterford eventually settled into it a bit but we always looked comfortable. Stephen Molumphy got them a goal, and shortly after Shanahan went for a point when there was a goal on.

It was so unlike him,

I could hardly believe it. Even though Waterford came back into it some of their players started arguing with the sideline. When I saw that happening I knew we'd ride the game out. Their heads were gone, pointing fingers before we'd even reached half-time.

We were actually only four points up at half-time, 2-9 to 1-8, which wasn't great considering how clear we pulled ahead at one stage. Still the message in the dressing-room was very simple.

I told the lads to just keep at it, that Waterford couldn't live with us like this. Get back out there, more of the same please.

And while Waterford had started to perform better towards the end of the first-half they were all over the place after the restart, hitting some erratic wides. It just wasn't going their way, and much of that was down to how hard our lads were working. The Waterford players always had to make pressure decisions. Ryan scored another goal which put us seven clear again.

Ten minutes into the second-half they took off Mullane, who Hickey had held scoreless. I was shocked. Mullane had been sick during the week and wasn't going great but he could always produce a moment of magic. I'm not sure if Justin gave enough, if any thought, to the fact that that was a massive mental boost for our players.

It signalled that we had their number.

Their key forwards weren't delivering for them. The intensity of our play started to slip, which was always a danger. It's hard to keep that up for 70 plus minutes. We took off Sean O'Connor because we felt he had his job done, but Waterford started to creep back into it. We missed some chances that we really should have put way.

Shortly after O'Connor came off, Browne hit a point that left us just one point ahead. Then we got a penalty when Ken McGrath tackled Begley to the ground. Andrew O'Shaughnessy looked over at us.

He was seeking approval on whether to go for goal, thinking we might want him to play it safe and take his point.

You'd never doubt Shaughs.

Go for goal.

He buried it. From the puck out, there was a long clearance, the ball came to Brian Begley and we had another goal.

Game over.

It was a brilliant day. To think the same group of players had lost by 17 points to Clare a year previously. They had come so far in such a short space of time. I was immensely proud of them. I was proud that they even got that far, never mind putting in a performance like that to win the game.

I knew what it meant to them to prove so many people wrong and bring some joy and pride back to Limerick supporters. We had laid out a plan and the squad had performed out of their skin. The work rate was incredible to watch up close, and the shift that our defenders put in was just outstanding. Dan Shanahan had hit us for 3-3 just a few weeks beforehand, and now we had limited him to only 0-4.

So many of our players were outstanding on the day. O'Shaugnessy lit the place up and scored 2-7.

I was absolutely buzzing with excitement.

I was interviewed for RTÉ on the pitch just moments after the final whistle. What we had just achieved hadn't even began to sink in yet. One of the first questions put to me was that goals win games, and that we took our five goals well.

'We got five of them and Dan the Man got none,' I replied, with a massive smile on my face. It was a throwaway comment that just sort of came out in the moment. It didn't land too well with Waterford supporters.

I wouldn't mind, but many people didn't get the context. Shanahan had been torching defences that year, and we'd been burned ourselves in the Munster final. We had just become the first team to stop him scoring a goal all summer.

Keeping 'Dan the Man' quiet was something to be proud of.

Also, I had actually outlined how much we admired Waterford in the same sentence, but that was also lost on many people. If you watch the clip back, the full comment was… 'We got five of them and Dan the Man got none. But I'll tell you what, my heart goes out for Waterford. If we weren't there, we would have wished Waterford were in the All-Ireland, but that's the way sport goes.'

Later on, I was asked if I thought that was the end for Waterford.

'I hope not,' I said.

'Genuinely, my heart goes out to them. They've tried for the last number of years and so near and yet so far.'

Still, it was the 'Dan the Man' comment that made all the headlines. Dan himself took fierce offence to it. He brought out a book a few years later and fairly ridiculed me in it. He said that I had nothing to do with Limerick's resurgence at the time, and that it was all down to Gary Kirby.

I'm not sure why he took it the wrong way. I thought that it was clear that I meant what I said as a compliment. We had worked on a plan to nullify Waterford's greatest threat, had successfully implemented that plan, and I was proud of it. If someone had boasted about keeping me scoreless when I was playing, I'd be honoured.

I would have taken it as a sign that they held me in high esteem.

Dan obviously didn't see things the same way.

Comments like that can get so easily blown out of proportion anyway. I was a bit surprised by the reaction to it. I had kind of forgotten what I had said as soon as the interview had ended. I was still caught up in the emotion of it all.

I've always felt that you're interviewed too soon after a match.

I was still on the pitch when I made that comment, which is madness really. We were all as high as kites. It was wild.

There were supporters teeming out onto the pitch behind us, and me trying to make sense of what had just happened live on national television? You're trying to take it all in and before you know it there is a microphone shoved in front of your face, asking you to describe a feeling that you actually haven't had any time to appreciate yourself yet.

Still, it did make good TV.

I'm sure if it was someone else, I would have enjoyed sitting at home watching it on my couch. I'd make no apologies for taking such happiness from a great win. That's what we're all in it for.

A few people asked me what those days felt like, and honest to God, they were even more enjoyable than when I was a player. I'm not entirely sure why that is. I think as a manger you're maybe a bit more tuned in to everything that is going on around you. Things like the buzz of the crowd.

I was turning around and cheering at the Limerick supporters during that game, getting caught up in the moment and soaking it all up. On the pitch you'd always be focusing on the next task. You also want the team to win more because you're more aware of just how much all the lads are doing behind the scenes. I wanted the team to do well because I liked them all.

We had a really good bond. I did an interview with Marty Morrissey afterwards and he asked me how winning an All-Ireland now would compare to winning it as a player in 1973? I told him that it would mean more to me if we could do it with this group, and I meant it.

I went into the Waterford dressing-room and they were obviously hugely disappointed. I told them that while we'd treasure the day, we took no great joy in beating them.

They were like ourselves, or Clare, a team often on the cusp that are trying to make that breakthrough. I told them that they were just like us, and for teams like us the aim is to beat Tipperary and Kilkenny.

I had meant what I said about wanting them to win the All-Ireland if it wasn't us. I really enjoyed some of the hurling they played, and they had some fantastic hurlers. I wished them well and told them they'd be back.

I went over to shake Justin's hand and he didn't even look up at me.

He just sat there slumped on a bench. He looked miserable. I could see he felt that he got it wrong on the sideline. He had been very quiet throughout the game actually.

I said my goodbyes and headed back to our own lads.

« CHAPTER 20 »

IT'S AMAZING HOW quickly the next task suddenly comes into focus.

An All-Ireland final.

Kilkenny.

Cody.

They had beaten us well in Nowlan Park during the league, but we were by no means afraid of them. That said, they were the best team that I had ever seen play the game.

No question.

They were at their absolute peak at that stage.

AS USUAL, WE sat down to pick out their key men.

Tommy Walsh and Henry Shefflin, obviously.

Then you had JJ Delaney and Jackie Tyrell.

Eddie Brennan too.

The pen kept moving across the page. Cha Fitzpatrick, Noel Hickey, Brian Hogan, Martin Comerford, Eoin Larkin, Aidan Fogarty... it was going to be a busy few weeks.

We studied them in detail, pouring over their games trying to find any hint of a weakness to take advantage of, or a habit we could try to exploit. There was a perception that Kilkenny just went out there and hurled away, but there was always real thought behind how they approached the game.

They always targeted a weak link in the opposition.

We tried to work out who they would go after in our team. Seamus Hickey had been performing brilliantly for us, but he was only 19. Of all our defenders, he was the most raw. As good a hurler as Seamus was, that's who I would target as an opposition manager.

'Let's see what this young fella is really made of!'

Mark O'Riordan had generally been on the bench for us that season. He had played corner-back for the Limerick team that reached the Munster football finals in 2003 and 2004. He was a real tough bit of stuff, a tenacious defender.

We looked at the type of hurling that Eddie Brennan played, and we felt that it wouldn't suit Hickey. Brennan would take you on, and Hickey wasn't at the stage where we felt that he could properly handle that yet. If Brennan only got the better of you once or twice across 70 minutes, it was enough for him to really influence a game.

We thought that O'Riordan was probably better suited to deal with Brennan. We seriously discussed dropping Hickey for the final, but we all came to the same conclusion. You just couldn't drop him after the performance he had put in the last day, when he did such an excellent job of keeping Mullane under wraps.

I thought marking Mullane was the toughest test for any defender.

So, we stuck by him.

Those weeks before the game flew by. Training was great. The lads were mighty. The application and focus was exactly what we wanted to see.

Paul O'Connell came in to talk to the squad and he was brilliant. He spoke about what to expect in terms of playing in front of a crowd of that size. He spoke about how it can make you feel and underlined the importance of staying focused.

He said some of the Ireland lads found it can help to put your head down and try blank it out. Overall his message was very positive. He didn't come in and say, 'You need to do this or that'. Instead, he pointed out all that the lads had achieved up to that point and said to keep doing what we were doing.

It was all very positive. He praised the way we had gone about things.

He was great, and you could see the confidence the lads got from hearing someone of his stature saying such positive things about us. He didn't say a single negative word. I've met him a couple of times down the years and he's a very nice fella, a very impressive man.

We didn't get anyone else in because I didn't want to overdo it.

I was wary of having lots of new voices because I felt that can send the message that we needed a load of help to get over the final hurdle. I wanted the lads to be in the mindset that more of the same would do us just fine. That we deserved to be there and we were good enough to beat Kilkenny.

There was one fella from Cork who wanted to come up and give some talk about the mental side of things. He wanted to play music in the background while he spoke to the lads and do different mental techniques, but I shot that down.

This was the biggest game of our lives, but that was it.

It was just another game.

No bother to us. Gary Kirby had his own All-Ireland final experiences obviously, as did I. We felt we managed the run-in well.

YOU TRY TO switch off from the hype around the place but it's impossible. We knew that the rest of the country saw this as a special final. All the neutrals wanted us to win, just as they would have with Waterford if they had reached the final.

Everyone loves an underdog.

A few days after the semi-final the letters started dropping through the front door at home, all well-wishers from around the country. I received letters from Donegal, Sligo, Armagh, you name it.

All addressed… Richie Bennis, Patrickswell, Co Limerick.

That was enough to find me. In a sense you feel as if you're representing more than Limerick. I wanted us to win for all the counties trying to reach that level. Nobody thought we'd be in an All-Ireland final that year.

I wanted to show everyone that with a bit of hard work, you can do anything.

THE OVERWHELMING SENSE on the morning of the game was one of calm. We had the breakfast, made our way out to Croke Park and everything seemed rosy.

It was exciting.

The lads got ready and even as the clock ticked closer to throw-in, everyone seemed reasonably confident about the task ahead. There was the odd bit of natural nerves I'm sure, but I always thought that if you weren't a small bit nervous before a big game, you weren't right.

There was no major team talk.

We had done all the talking we needed to. I had explained to the lads as best as I could what to expect when they ran out. I thought about being in their position 34 years previously. I could still picture it so clearly.

That roar would still give you goosebumps.

I told them to just concentrate on the game when they marched around with the band beforehand. Think about your job. Think about the man you're marking.

I told them to avoid looking up into the crowd.

The problem was that it was very hard to prepare them for what they went out and met. Kilkenny ran out first and got a big cheer.

Nothing special.

Then we got the knock on the door and off we headed. I expected an almighty roar when the lads emerged from the tunnel but what greeted us was off the scale. I'll never forget the noise of it.

It felt like the ground was shaking.

One of the staff in the tunnel came up to me and said that in 45 years of working in Croke Park, he had never heard the like of it.

Then we got out there and we got another jolt.

The sea of green was unreal. There were green jerseys everywhere. I don't know how they did it but the Limerick supporters seemed to make up 75 per cent of the crowd. I thought I was well prepared for it but in truth it got to me a little bit.

It took me about 10 minutes after we went out to settle and properly assess the thing. We had heard the stories that it was going to be a massive Limerick crowd but this was beyond belief.

The noise must have affected our lads, and I remember thinking that Kilkenny would be loving it, thinking they were there to spoil our party.

If our lads needed any reminder just how big the occasion was, they got it.

ALL-IRELANDS FINALS are funny. It's this big event that you spend so much time planning for, and then when it arrives it all goes by in such a flash. Best laid plans can go out the window in a matter of seconds.

We knew Kilkenny were heavily fancied, but we were quietly confident in ourselves. How could we not be with the summer we had had?

The biggest surprise in the Kilkenny team was that Willie O'Dywer started at corner-forward ahead of Richie Power, but it didn't disrupt anything that we had planned to do. Henry Shefflin won the toss, so we were playing into the Hill for the first half.

It was a frantic start to the game. From the throw-in there was immediate chaos, with about six Limerick bodies and eight Kilkenny bodies around the ball. They eventually gathered it and the first ball was pumped down towards our goal.

This would be Seamus Hickey's first test of the day.

After a brief scramble he won a free out. Grand, a nice comfortable start for him, his first possession dealt with just fine.

Shefflin scored their first point from a free.

Eddie Brennan then caught Stephen Lucey high and was fortunate not to get booked. We had to take Lucey off temporarily. I'd be happy enough if that was the only damage Brennan did on the day.

Kilkenny aimed a couple of aerial balls in towards him in the first few minutes but nothing came of them, and we were satisfied with the way things were going. Lucey came back in shortly before Jackie Tyrell sent another ball down towards Brennan. We gathered it up and Lucey cleared it, but it sailed out for a Kilkenny lineball around the halfway, down in front of us on the Hogan Stand side.

Unfortunately, in the next few moments all of our fears about Hickey on Brennan played out before our eyes.

Cha Fitzpatrick aimed the sideline in towards Brennan on the near side.

He beat Hickey to the ball, looped him on the endline and struck it low into the net.

Nine minutes played.

1-2 to 0-0.

ALARM BELLS WENT off straight away.

We knew it could get ugly, but you couldn't pull Hickey out of that game, of all games, that early. He might have been in for a rough afternoon, but even if we had just switched him off Brennan, it would have completely shattered his confidence.

It would have sent a bad message to the rest of the team as well.

It would have looked like we were panicking, or being too reactionary. We backed him to settle into it, but at that stage we all knew that we should have gone with our first instinct and started O'Riordan instead.

We had got the call wrong and had paid dearly for it.

FROM THE PUCK-OUT Kilkenny won the ball again, and sent it in where this time Shefflin was waiting. That was the problem with Kilkenny.

Even if you have Brennan taken care of, there's Shefflin to step in instead.

They just had threats everywhere. Shefflin caught it ahead of Lucey, turned and was able to negotiate enough room for himself to flick the ball in for their second goal.

Two goals in the space of a minute.

Eoin Larkin followed up with a point. From five attacks, they had five scores.

2-3 to 0-0.

An absolute disaster.

ANDREW O'SHAUGHNESSY FINALLY got us off the mark with a point from a free after 12 minutes. We got our first point from play from Donal O'Grady after 15 minutes. Seanie O'Connor then made it three in-a-row for us.

Gradually we were settling into the game.

We traded a few points.

Kilkenny were still hungry for goals. Hickey made a brilliant diving block to deflect a goal-bound shot from Brennan over the bar. Cody then brought on Richie Power for Willie O'Dwyer. We went almost 10 minutes without scoring, and they were doing a good job of keeping O'Shaughnessy under wraps.

At half-time we trailed 2-10 to 0-8, which was by no means a disaster given how the first 10 minutes had played out.

We retreated from the storm.

I was actually happy with how the lads were in the dressing-room. They were still focused and still believed the game was there to be won. They knew that seven points in hurling is nothing, and we reinforced that.

We made sure we were calm in delivering our own message.

There was no shouting or banging tables or anything like that. Gary said a few words about the times he had found himself in a similar situation down the years. He was on a Limerick team that were 10 points down in the 1996 Munster final, but they brought it back to a draw and won the replay.

The lads nodded along as he spoke.

Despite a disastrous start to the game there were no heads down.

I told them to just keep at it.

I told them we could catch them.

Shefflin couldn't continue after half-time due to a knee injury, which had to be a big mental blow to them. We started the second-half really strongly. We scored the first two points.

At that stage there was six points between us.

We hurled quite well for the rest of the game but Kilkenny just kept us at bay. They moved nine up, and then Ollie Moran struck a fine goal just on 50 minutes to cut it back to six again. He was the first to react to a loose ball, flicked it up and rifled it past PJ Ryan.

A real classy finish.

Ollie had been hurling with Limerick for 10 years. I was delighted for him.

We scored plenty of good points, and every time we did the crowd got right behind us again. The noise was incredible after Ollie's goal.

You'd have sworn we were in the lead.

The whole time I was keeping an eye on Cody down the line.

I could get a sense of how the Kilkenny players felt by watching his movements. He's usually very calm, but it's easy to be calm when you're winning. He has little signs when his teams are under pressure.

During the second-half I could see him pacing around a bit more or spitting into his hands and rubbing them together.

You want to see that as the opposition manager.

He knew we weren't dead and buried. He knew that we should have been.

Lovely, I thought to myself.

KILKENNY JUST KEPT chipping away though.

We'd pull them in a little bit and then it was an eight-point gap again before we knew it. We had good chances too.

O'Shaughnessy struck a fierce free at goal but JJ Delaney produced a superb block. Most days it would have flown into the net. We picked off a few points and brought it back to five.

O'Shaughnessy then found himself in front of goal without his hurley, which he says was held. He kicked the sliothar towards goal with his right boot but Tyrell managed to dive across and block the shot with his stick.

We couldn't beat them at hurling, or football. That would have made it a two-point game. That was the chance.

We were hanging in there. They went nine minutes without a score. Richie Power ended that dry spell.

We missed a few more chances and Brennan struck a point.

It petered out from there. We pushed for a late goal but were getting nowhere. O'Shaugnessy tried to barge through in the last minute but the attack broke down. Kilkenny went up the other end and Brennan scored a point.

They started celebrating then.

Cody turned around and hugged Ned Quinn, the Kilkenny county chairman.

The referee blew it up about 20 seconds later. Cody threw his arms into the air and found Shefflin, the pair of them embracing as the photographers whirled around to get the money shot. Their players leapt around the place while some of ours fell to the ground. Others stared into space.

I walked out onto the pitch and waded through the Kilkenny supporters that had run out to see their heroes. I wasn't heading in any particular direction, just hugging any of our lads that I could find, congratulating any of the Kilkenny boys I passed.

I almost viewed the match in two different parts.

Those first 10 minutes were a disaster for us, but we gave them a right good go once we had settled. They got off to the type of start that we had needed if we were going to beat them.

2-3 to 0-0 after 10 minutes.

There wasn't a team in the country that would have caught them after that. We had actually out-scored them after, 1-15 to 0-17, but the damage had been done.

That was what Kilkenny did to teams.

They had the ability to kill you off before you even realised what was happening. The intensity of their play was just on another level to anything that we had experienced, and their discipline as a unit was remarkable.

And even though our lads were fully up for the challenge, and felt that they could win, there was no escaping the fact that the whole occasion of an All-Ireland final was new to them. For Kilkenny, I'd say being in an All-Ireland final was a minimum expectation at the start of each season.

On reflection I also thought that our semi-final against Waterford had taken so much out of our lads that to perform an even bigger upset three weeks later was just a step too far. If they had managed to do it, it would have been one of the most unlikely All-Ireland wins ever.

But that day, when it mattered most, there were loads of little moments that just didn't fall our way. Again, that's just the way it goes sometimes. It wasn't easy to take, but I certainly wasn't bitter about the defeat.

THE ONLY ASPECT of what happened that day that really disappointed me was I felt the performances of some of our players wasn't really picked up on due to the nature of the defeat. Some of our guys actually played really well, but nobody remembers that of course. That's just the way sport is at that level, but I wished they had got a bit more recognition.

It was a low-key end to what had been a marvellous effort by the lads that year.

I was heartbroken for Ollie Moran.

Ollie scored 1-3 that day, which is a fine tally in any final. He was a tremendous leader that season for us. A manager's dream.

I must admit, it was Gary's decision to move him into the forwards. Ollie had always been an outstanding hurler, but Gary made the decision to push him up the field. He could really influence a game from there. He provided some massive moments for us throughout the summer.

While there was no shame in being beaten by that Kilkenny team, I don't think we got the credit we deserved for that performance. Seven points wasn't a huge beating by that Kilkenny team. If we met any other team that day, we'd have won the All-Ireland, but nobody was stopping Kilkenny in 2007.

We probably weren't alone in that mindset.

I went into the Kilkenny dressing-room after the game and told them that the best team had won, I wished them the best of luck going forward, and said that it had been an honour for me to manage a team against them in an All-Ireland final because they were one of the greatest teams I had ever seen.

Cody came into our dressing-room as well and he spoke very well.

He told our lads about being part of the Kilkenny team that lost the 1973 final to us, but that they came back and beat us the following year. He said there was no reason that our lads couldn't come back and do the exact same thing to them next year.

It was a classy speech.

I'd have great time for him and found him a genuine, sound man.

We had our banquet in the Red Cow Hotel that night and it was actually fairly jolly and upbeat. We felt that we had come from nowhere to reach an All-Ireland final, and we had beaten some really strong teams along the way. Everyone had felt that Waterford were the second-best team in the country. That meant that for the first time in 1973, Limerick had beaten one of the top five teams in Croke Park.

That was something to be proud of. Limerick had played in All-Ireland semi-finals in 1994 and 1996, but had beaten Antrim comfortably on both occasions. Antrim were a decent side, but nobody would have considered them a top five team.

It also didn't feel like the end of something.

Even that night in the Red Cow, I was thinking to myself that we could be back here in 12 months time with the Liam MacCarthy Cup taking pride of place.

We were still in good health.

I was hungry for more. My contract was for two years with an option for a third, but until that point, I hadn't actually thought about whose option it was, mine or theirs.

I'd find out the following year.

EVEN BEFORE WE pucked a ball the following season, I could sense that it wasn't going to be our year.

One of the biggest issues was that we had no consistent place to train.

In 2007 we had been able to train in the Gaelic Grounds. Now the pitch had fallen into too bad of a state for us to use, so we were out on our backsides. We found ourselves going from field to field each week.

We were constantly ringing around different clubs, asking if we could use their pitches? It wasn't fair on the lads. Playing senior county hurling is a huge commitment, and the lads were being let down. The players would be off at work or in college, going about their day, and they wouldn't know where training was going to be on that evening.

You might not have a training pitch secured until 5.0 pm that day.

Then it was a case of letting everyone know as quickly as possible so they could make the necessary arrangements to get to wherever it was we were pitching up for a session.

It was lunacy.

I felt so bad about the whole way things were being done.

We weren't the only team having some issues behind the scenes. Clare beat Waterford in the Munster championship, and you could see that Waterford were slipping. That was the day that Shanahan was substituted and didn't shake Justin McCarthy's hand when he was coming off the field. It ended up being Justin's last match.

In fairness he had probably brought them as far as he could have by that stage.

We were due to play Clare next, and we all thought that we would beat them with little problem. We probably should have too, but they scored two goals which allowed them to pull away. It was becoming more and more clear to me that we weren't right.

There wasn't the same enthusiasm in training, and the whole atmosphere had changed. The energy wasn't the same.

I started to feel that they were the type of lads that needed someone to win it for them on the sideline. They weren't going to go out and win it for themselves.

In 2007 we knew the players had the drive to do it for themselves and push the whole thing along, but now they were looking for us to do more for them. You see that with teams sometimes. How many counties turn to an outside manger with a great track record, but their own performances or effort doesn't change?

We saw it in Limerick with Na Piarsaigh recently. They brought in Michael Ryan, an All-Ireland winner with Tipp, at the start of 2019 and lost the Limerick county final to Patrickswell. It was the first time in three years they weren't county champions, and you could see the drive wasn't really there.

The problem with motivation is that it is a two-way thing.

The players need to be doing enough to motivate a manger to motivate them. In 2008, our lads looked like a group that were losing interest.

WE DREW OFFALY in the qualifiers, and they beat us in the Gaelic Grounds. It was another complete mess.

There had been another match scheduled for the stadium on the Sunday, so the county board wanted us to play up in Kilmallock instead. Obviously, I was having none of it. In my mind, Limerick's championship home games were played at the Gaelic Grounds.

Full stop.

No conversation necessary.

I could scarcely believe we were even being asked to move. We didn't actually get the green light to play it in the Gaelic Grounds until the morning of the game.

That was typical of the lack of proper preparation that we had to deal with all year. I could fully understand why lads were getting cheesed off. How could they be expected to keep giving it their all when their own county board didn't give a toss?

We had all these talented, committed hurlers, who had shown what they were capable of the previous summer, and the county board had no belief in them. Everything was a struggle. It was a real shame for the players, but it was also unfair on the supporters who were paying money and travelling around to see a team that weren't getting proper support from the powers-that-be.

We were due to train in Kilmallock about a week before the Offaly game, and when we got there, there was an under-8 game on.

So, we all sat around and watched this under-8 game until we could have the pitch. That was how the previous year's beaten All-Ireland finalists were preparing for a championship match. Our trainer was getting increasingly disgusted with the whole thing as the weeks dragged on.

He was investing so much time into meticulously planning everything for the lads, only to get dumped into scenarios like that.

It looked as though we were going through the motions against Offaly. Lads looked tired and disinterested. It wasn't the way I knew them, and it was awful to see.

We lost 3-19 to 0-18.

Shortly after that my job as manager was up for grabs again.

My extra year was no longer on the table. It didn't surprise me. I knew before the Offaly game that Justin McCarthy was on-board to take over. I had heard from a reliable source that he had been approached. Even though we had beaten his Waterford team the previous year, he was still highly regarded as a manager.

And rightly so, as he did great things with that Waterford team. The Limerick job was a totally different task though. Justin got his hands on that

Waterford team when they were young, whereas the Limerick squad was at the other end of the age scale.

Despite all the setbacks we had had in 2008 I would have done another year as manager. I knew the potential was there if we could only sort out all the nonsense off the pitch. We still had enough quality players to achieve something, and I had a great backroom team around me.

It was all getting very professional.

The only problem was that some of the playing group were coming to the end of their careers. They had been together a long time as a group. Most of them had been playing alongside each other since the Limerick teams that won three successive under-21 All-Irelands between 2000-2002.

THINGS STARTED TO quickly unravel.

The Tuesday after the Offaly match, I got a call from one of the local Limerick journalists. He told me that there was a strong rumour some of the lads had been out drinking the night before the match.

I told him if those rumours were true, then those players had let me down. But I had no knowledge of whether the rumours were true or not.

I still don't.

I've never spoken to anyone who has been able to categorically say that it had happened. The headline that went out had me saying I had been let down by my players. The quote was taken out of context.

Limerick were said to have had a bit of a drinking culture, but it was only two or three players. That's all it takes to tarnish a whole groups' name. It was by no means an issue with the whole squad, and it certainly wasn't something I had to devote any time to try stop.

I knew I could trust the vast majority of the players.

And it wasn't a case that we enforced any kind of drink ban on the players. Some lads would have the occasional pint, and that was fine.

We had no problem with that.

Sure Jesus, there isn't a hope in hell that we could have reached an All-Ireland final, given the calibre of the opposition that we beat along the way, if we had lads out sinking pints during the week or after games. It was very rare that a player would even miss a training session.

Even in 2008 when the schedule was a mess and players were only finding out where we were training at 5.0 pm, nobody failed to show up.

They were a fantastic group to manage.

The only problem was that if a player was seen having a pint, it could cause all sorts of rumours and get blown out of proportion. I remember at one stage Brian Murray, our goalkeeper, was accused of being out drinking.

Brian was from Patrickswell, so I'd have known him well anyway.

I'd be amazed if Brian drank 10 pints over the course of two months.

If you lost a game, and someone spotted you drinking a pint, then you ended up being accused of drinking. If you had won, it was seen as well-deserved... 'Sure aren't they entitled to unwind after beating such and such'.

It's tough on players, and it has only gotten worse.

Some lads now would be out, and they're afraid to even carry a drink for their friend, or partner or whatever, in case someone accuses them. I would have often spoken to Joe McKenna too, and he was positive that there was no drink culture under his watch either. I know that there certainly isn't any problem under John Kiely now.

JUSTIN MCCARTHY DIDN'T have it easy after me, and I knew he wouldn't. Justin is a Cork man of course, and it's always a bit more difficult to manage a county that you're not from.

Everything you do comes with the scrutiny of being 'an outsider', and it's easy to lob the 'sure what does he know about Limerick' thing at them too.

He got rid of a lot of lads that had been hurling with Limerick for years. He was right to do it, but he went about it the wrong way. I was planning on doing the same thing, but I would have met each player face to face and explained the situation.

I think you have to give players that courtesy, and show them that respect. My plan was to bring in a raft of new players in order to build up the panel in pre-season, and then make decisions on who would be kept in the squad based on that.

Justin just swung an axe.

You're always likely to fall foul of some of the fellows that stay on when you approach things in such a fashion. It certainly didn't help his case when it appeared in the paper, and suddenly the whole county knew about it. It immediately painted a picture of Justin as this cold character who had come in to shake things up.

His way or the highway. I got the impression that he lost a lot of the dressing-room early on. You saw that later with some of the things lads came out and said about training sessions.

After 2009 he got rid of 12 players, including Andrew O'Shaughnessy, Mark O'Riordan, Stephen Lucey, Donie Ryan, Niall Moran and Mike O'Brien. Most of them found out via a report in the Irish Examiner.

A handful more walked away a few months later.

I felt bad seeing the lads being treated that way. Whatever was going on behind the scenes, I knew what they had given to Limerick hurling. I know how much it meant to them.

It was a bad way for that group to break up.

It made me appreciate just how good our time in charge had been.

I ended up the best of friends with every player on the squad. I can say that with my hand on my heart. We got on great. It's a lovely way to be able to look back on that time. We didn't get the prize we wanted, but we certainly gave it our all, and had a hell of a good time along the way.

It's great to be able to look back on it all and smile.

And have the great game smile back at me!

MORE
GREAT
SPORTS BOOKS
FROM
HEROBOOKS

ANOTHER BRILLIANT LIMERICK STORY!

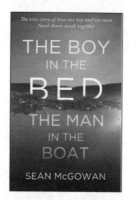

The Boy in the Bed
The Man in the Boat
Sean McGowan: An Autobiography

Sean McGowan is 'The Boy in the Bed' and 'The Man in the Boat', and he was born and still lives in Limerick, with his wife Lorraine, and their four children, Rachael, Daniel, Patrick and Chloe.

Now in his early 40s, Sean remains an asthmatic.

As a young boy, Sean spent four and a half years in a bed, in and out, in hospital and in his home in Limerick, fighting a long and cruel battle with chronic asthma, and a battle for life which, repeatedly, he came so close to losing.

Sean, finally, won that war. For now!

On January 4, 2010, Sean left La Gomera in the Canary Islands, which was the start line to the Woodvale Ocean Rowing Race. It was a race that almost cost him his life, as he met with wretched luck and the most violent of storms recorded in the Atlantic in the last two decades, but Sean and 'Tess' (24 feet long and six feet at its widest point) somehow survived 118 days, one hour, and 14 minutes at sea, before finally reaching the finish line of English Harbour in Antigua.

Just the two of them – roughly 50 days late!

Authors: Sean McGowan with Liam Hayes
Print Price: €20.00
Ebook: €10.00
ISBN: 9781910827116

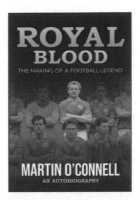

Royal Blood
Martin O'Connell: An Autobiography

Three times All-Ireland winner, Martin O'Connell was crowned the prince of wing backs in 2000 when he was selected on the GAA's Team of the Millennium, and had a postage stamp issued in his honour.

This honour also stamped O'Connell's name down in Meath football history as the greatest of the greats.

As a Meath footballer, O'Connell truly had Royal Blood. He was a central player on Sean Boylan's 1987 and 88 All-Ireland winning teams, and then remained with Boylan to win a third All-Ireland in 1996 in an infamous replayed final against Mayo.

Now, O'Connell reveals the inside story of those battling years, and explains how it might never have happened after he quit the Meath team in the mid 80s. But his love of the game brought him back.

In addition to his three All-Irelands, Martin O'Connell won six Leinster titles and three National league titles and in 1996 was named Footballer of the Year. After retiring from the Meath team he continued playing football with St Michael's, his club and his first love in football, until he was 42 years old.

Authors: Martin O'Connell and David Sheehan
Print Price: €20.00
Ebook: €10.00
ISBN: 9781910827109

Available on
Amazon
Apple
Kobo
And all good online stores

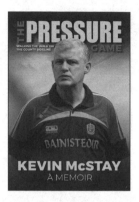

The Pressure Game
Kevin McStay: An Autobiography

FOR THE FIRST time one of the top GAA managers in the country has revealed the inside story of what it's like to 'Walk the Walk on a County Sideline'. Former Mayo Allstar footballer Kevin McStay gave up 20 years of working as a commentator and analyst on RTE's Sunday Game to take up the position of Roscommon team manager in 2016.

The whole country watched to see how he would survive on the sideline – and how he would face up to the pressures of facing Jim's Gavin's Dublin, Mayo and Kerry and Tyrone, on the toughest stage in Gaelic football.

In his three years in charge, McStay led Roscommon to a Connacht title in 2017 and a prized place in the Super 8s in 2018 before quitting the job. He has now returned to the RTE broadcasting booth.

This is the amazing inside story of the *The Pressure Game.*

Authors: Kevin McStay with Liam Hayes
Print Price: €20.00
Ebook: €10.00
ISBN: 9781910827086

Available on

Amazon
Apple
Kobo
And all good online stores

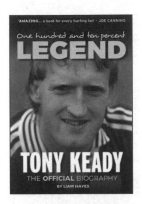

One Hundred and Ten Percent Legend
Tony Keady: The Official Biography

WHEN TONY KEADY died suddenly in August of 2017, at just 53 years of age, a whole county mourned and the rest of the country stopped in its tracks to say goodbye to a legend of the game of hurling.

Except Tony Keady was more than a legend.

In 1988, after leading Galway to a second All-Ireland title in succession, he was crowned the greatest hurler in Ireland. He was 25 years of age and there was nobody like him, nobody to touch him in the maroon No.6 shirt.

But, four years later, and still not 30, after being wrongly banned for 12 months by the GAA, he was also discarded by his own county and refused a maroon jersey the very last time he walked out onto Croke Park behind the Galway team.

A few months before his death, Tony Keady visited Liam Hayes and told him he wished to tell his own story. He felt it was time, but tragically time was not on Tony's side. One month after he died Galway won the All-Ireland title for the first time since 1988, and 80,000 people rose from their seats in the sixth minute of the game to applaud and remember a man who was more than a legend

Tony's wife, Margaret and his daughter, Shannon and his three boys, Anthony, Harry and Jake, decided to finish telling the story of a father and a hurler who always asked those around him for '110%.

Author: Liam Hayes
Price: €20.00
ISBN: 9781910827048

A Land of Men and Giants
The Tony Doran Autobiography

WEXFORD'S ALL-IRELAND winning hero Tony Doran was a giant in the game of hurling through the 1960s, 70s and 80s, at a time when full-forwards were ordered to plunder goals.

In his 19 years and 187 appearances as a Wexford hurler, Tony Doran successfully went for goal 131 times.

But Doran also played against giants from Kilkenny, Tipperary and Cork, and so many other counties, at a time when the game of hurling tested the wits and the courage of every man on the field.

Some of these men became giants.

A Land of Men and Giants is the story told by Tony Doran of a life spent living and competing against legendary men and true giants of the game.

A Land of Men and Giants: The Autobiography of Tony Doran is edited by award-winning writer and author Liam Hayes.

Authors: Tony Doran with Liam Hayes
Print Price: €20.00
ISBN: 9781910827031

Available on
Amazon

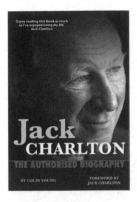

Jack Charlton
The Authorised Biography

AS ONE OF the true legends of Irish and English football, Jack Charlton was a man both loved and feared, but now the people who have lived with him all of his life introduce the real 'Big Jack' in this brilliant authorised biography which is presented in a foreword by Jack himself.

For the first time Jack's wife and family, his teammates as a World Cup winner with England in 1966, and his players during his management years with Middlesbrough, Sheffield Wednesday, Newcastle, and Ireland tell their stories of the man who dominated their lives.

Graeme Souness, Chris Waddle, and Peter Beardsley amongst others, are joined by Mick McCarthy, Niall Quinn and the greatest footballers who played under Big Jack for 10 years as Ireland team boss.

This is the most personable, inviting and intimate account of Jack Charlton's life, and the book contains photographs published for the first time from Jack and Pat Charlton's personal collection.

Jack Charlton: The Authorised Biography is written by former Daily Mail Northern Football Correspondent, Colin Young.

Authors: Colin Young
Print Price: €20.00
ISBN: 9781910827017

Available on
Amazon

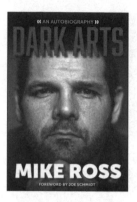

Dark Arts
Mike Ross: An Autobiography

FOR THE FIRST time, Mike Ross brings sports fans into the dark heart of the professional game of rugby union. Ross is recognised as the greatest scrummager in Irish rugby history – and the man who was the foundation stone for the beginning of the Joe Schmidt era, which saw Leinster win back-to-back Heineken Cups and Ireland become the greatest team in Europe.

But Mike Ross might never have been a professional rugby player. He did not turn pro until he was 26 years of age. And he spent three years learning his trade at the toughest end of the game with Harlequins in England before coming home at 30, and chasing the dream of an Irish jersey.

Ross would play 61 times for Ireland, and over 150 times for Leinster. His story is one of big dreams and amazing courage, on and off the field.

He writes about the good times and the hardest times, facing the true beasts of the professional game every weekend. And he writes about his own life, and the suicide of his younger brother, Andrew at 16 years of age with an honesty and compassion that is rewarding for everyone who has experienced the sudden death of a loved one and has to rebuild their lives.

Authors: Mike Ross with Liam Hayes
Print Price: €20.00
Ebook: €10.00
ISBN: 9781910827048

Available on
Amazon
Apple
Kobo
And all good online stores